ANALYSIS OF TRANSFERENCE
VOLUME II
STUDIES OF NINE AUDIO-RECORDED
PSYCHOANALYTIC SESSIONS

ANALYSIS OF TRANSFERENCE
VOLUME II

STUDIES OF NINE AUDIO-RECORDED
PSYCHOANALYTIC SESSIONS

MERTON M. GILL
and
IRWIN Z. HOFFMAN

Psychological Issues
Monograph 54

INTERNATIONAL UNIVERSITIES PRESS, INC.
New York

Library of Congress Cataloging in Publication Data

Second printing, 1983

Gill, Merton Max, 1914-
    Analysis of transference.

    (Psychological issues ; monograph 53-54)
    Vol. 2 by Merton M. Gill and Irwin Z. Hoffman also
has title: Studies of nine audio-recorded psycho-
analytic sessions.
    Bibliography: v. 1, p.   ; v. 2, p.
    Includes indexes.
    1. Transference (Psychology) 2. Transference
(Psychology)—Case studies. I. Hoffman, Irwin Z.
II. Title. III. Series. [DNLM: 1. Transference
(Psychology) W1 PS572 monograph 53-54 / WM 62 G475a]
RC489.T73G57 1982   616.89'17   81-23654
ISBN 0-8236-0139-0 (v. 1)   AACR2
ISBN 0-8236-0140-4 (v. 2)

Manufactured in the United States of America

CONTENTS

ACKNOWLEDGMENTS

We are grateful to the patients and therapists who have permitted us to use this material. We hope that the benefits resulting from making it public will justify this yielding of their privacy. Although we are responsible for these particular annotations, we wish to thank the colleagues and students with whom we have studied many audio-recorded sessions for their helpful contributions to our thinking. The work was supported in part by Research Grant #30731 from the National Institute of Mental Health.

INTRODUCTION

The psychoanalytic literature abounds with case studies and anecdotal reports of clinical phenomena. The advantages and disadvantages of the case study method for building and testing clinical theory are well known. On the one hand, clinical concepts or hypotheses can be generated, illustrated, clarified, or modified on the basis of data selected for these purposes. In this respect, there is no question that the case study method has been and will continue to be indispensable to the development of psychoanalytic theory and technique. On the other hand, the very selection of the data, carried out by the same person whose viewpoint they are usually intended to support, inevitably casts doubt on the objectivity of the report. The reader, in the end, has no way of knowing whether there are other data that the author has wittingly or unwittingly left out of his account which either contradict the conclusions drawn or lend themselves to alternative explanations. Only by making the original data public can clinical hypotheses be subjected to the kind of critical scrutiny that science requires.

Psychoanalysis as an institution has been notoriously laggard in making the data gathered in the privacy of the consulting room available for such scrutiny. While other therapeutic modalities have been making use of audio and video recording for teaching and research purposes for many years (Rogers, 1942; Haggard, Hiken, and Isaacs, 1965; Gottschalk and Auerbach, 1966; Berger, 1978), with few exceptions (Will and Cohen, 1953; Luborsky, 1967; Wallerstein and Sampson, 1971; Dahl, 1974), psychoanalysts have been reluctant to dilute the guarantee of confidentiality that characterizes the analytic situation. This and other objections to tape recording have been taken up

1

in some detail and challenged elsewhere (Gill et al., 1968; Simon et al., 1970). But the fact remains that the case study approach has never been adequately complemented by either systematic research utilizing independent judges of the original data or by clinical reporting that gives the analytic and general scientific communities access to those data as a basis for evaluating the conclusions of the presenters or authors. This volume is a contribution toward filling this gap in the analytic literature. Its purpose will be well served if, in addition to illustrating concretely our particular point of view on technique and eliciting constructive criticism, it stimulates others to present their data in a similar format.

The sessions presented here were chosen to demonstrate particular issues, but that does not mean that they are especially atypical or unusual. We could readily have chosen many others. The sessions we have selected include some in which there is an attempt to carry out the principles we espouse, as well as some in which there is no such attempt—in other words, what we consider relatively good and relatively poor sessions. Our search for the ideal session has been futile, and we regret that we cannot offer a session that we are satisfied with as exemplary from start to finish. Here it must be remembered that we are presenting *entire* sessions. Although there are segments of some of the sessions—particularly within the last five—that we feel are exemplary, it seems unlikely that any therapist could maintain such a consistently high level of attention and insight that he would completely avoid the lapses that subsequent observers can pick up. Furthermore, our careful and repeated study of whole sessions has made it possible to perceive a hierarchy of transference themes, which the therapist would be unlikely to grasp fully in the ongoing situation. We are not saying that the technique in what we call "good" sessions could not be improved. On the contrary, a careful study of transcripts of sessions, however good the technique, can and should promote more skillful and consistent application of the principles we espouse.

Still, there are certain *a priori* reasons for pessimism about finding a session that is well conducted throughout. As we suggested above, one reason is that in studying a session at leisure it is always possible to see more in it than the therapist was able to see while he was conducting it. Thus, if an ideal session is defined as one in which the therapist sees all that subsequent observers do, it becomes something that is impossible to achieve. Even if one uses a less stringent criterion for an ideal session — namely, that all the critical or essential interpretations have been made in a tactful and timely way — it will still be very difficult to find such a session because observers will always disagree to a greater or lesser extent. Although we may obtain significant agreement on the major latent themes, questions of style, temperament, and other characteristics of the observer will lead to differences of opinion with regard to both content and timing of interventions. Just as it was argued in Volume I that there is no way to reach an externally judged unequivocally "correct" statement of the reality of the patient-therapist interaction, so too it follows that there is no unequivocally correct and all-inclusive intervention. Just as the patient's experience of a particular interaction can plausibly vary over a fairly wide range, so too can therapists' and observers' ideas about the nature of that experience. This follows simply from the fact that the manifest verbal and nonverbal behavior, whether of the patient or of the therapist, is always open to a variety of plausible interpretations as to its motivational determinants or meanings.

Here it is also important to emphasize that whenever we suggest a possible way in which the patient is experiencing the relationship, we are *not* implying that we believe the therapist should have made that explicit. Our annotations are intended to illuminate as much as we can about what is going on in the transference, not to stipulate either that all this should have been clear to the therapist or that the therapist should have attempted to make all this clear to the patient.

On the other hand, we do not wish to be misunderstood to be saying that anything the therapist does or does not do is equally acceptable. It will often be clear from our notes which interventions we considered good or bad and which interventions we believe should have been made in one form or another. In some instances, whether or not a suggested implicit meaning should have been interpreted at a particular moment is left open because we realize that differences in temperament and style, as well as knowledge of the case, are legitimate considerations in the timing of any intervention.

Our overall attitude toward what the therapist does or does not do is somewhat different, we believe, from a very common one in assessing analytic material. The usual view emphasizes the importance of the analyst's silence in permitting the patient's associations to emerge free of "contaminating" external influence. Silence, paradoxically, is also deemed effective in *inducing* the unfolding of a regressive transference neurosis (Macalpine, 1950). When interpretations are finally made, the patient's ensuing associations are not systematically scrutinized for indications of how the patient has preconsciously construed their interpersonal and possible countertransferential meanings (Langs, 1978). In our view, sustained silence is a very powerful stimulus, the effects of which will, by definition, pass uninterpreted and probably unrecognized as long as the analyst refrains from speaking. Consequently, we generally advocate a more active interpretive stance than is customary. Instead of the illusory aim of eliminating the analyst's interpersonal influence, we stress the importance of vigilance to disguised references by the patient to this influence, including whatever inadvertent interpersonal effects may stem from the act of interpreting itself.

We assume that the therapist who engages more freely with his patients will inevitably enact the role the patient assigns to him to a greater or lesser degree, without realizing he is doing so (Sandler, 1976). What we look for is not whether the therapist can avoid such enactment but whether he can gradually become aware of it and utilize that awareness in his interpretive work (cf. Racker, 1968, pp. 127–173, and Levenson, 1972, pp. 167–196). One of our characteristic findings in the sessions we studied was how often the very interpretation of a patient's experience of the relationship enacts what the patient takes as a plausible basis for that experience.

The term "transference" and the phrase "the patient's experience of the relationship" are used interchangeably throughout this monograph. In Volume I and elsewhere (Gill and Hoffman, 1982), the differences between our view of transference and the conventional one are spelled out at some length. While we would acknowledge that it may be useful conceptually to exclude certain aspects of the patient's experience of the relationship from "transference," what we are dealing with here are conflictual and resisted aspects of that experience which we feel it is safe to regard as transferential. In other words, these are aspects of the patient's experience that are probably governed by relatively rigid schemata associated with childhood wishes and childhood attempts to deal with early conflicts. In any case, resisted aspects of the patient's experience are what the analyst has to deal with on a moment-to-moment basis in any given session. What we reject categorically is the attempt to distinguish transference and nontransference on the grounds that the former has either no basis or only a trivial basis in current reality, whereas the latter is reality-based. On the contrary, the transference is usually organized around significant contributions from the analyst in the here-and-now, and the best transference interpretations usually include references to these contributions as plausibly construed by the patient.

We have chosen to present isolated sessions. A very different approach (with its own advantages and disadvantages) would have been to present a number of sessions from the same therapy, whether in sequence or not. We hope eventually to make this other kind of presentation, especially because we think it likely that, with regard to the technique we are attempting to assess, sessions from the same therapy will show a remarkable uniformity. This view is somewhat counter to the common view that to understand analytic material one needs access to the total therapy, sequentially, and from the beginning. In any case, our present purpose of illustrating relatively good and bad technique is best served by presenting diverse isolated sessions from a number of therapies.

By calling the sessions "isolated" we mean that we are providing neither historical background nor earlier or later material from the course of the therapy. Precisely because we want to show how much can be clear from the session alone, we have confined external data to the number of the session and the frequency with which the patient was being seen.

We realize that these isolated sessions shed no light on one of the major issues raised in Volume I, the role of genetic data in the resolution of the transference. While we have been able to present a little data bearing on the resolution of the transference in the here-and-now, an examination of the resolution of the transference through genetic interpretation would require longitudinal rather than cross-sectional studies.

Confidentiality is also more easily maintained by using isolated sessions. The publishing of verbatim material makes it more difficult to maintain confidentiality than is the case when presenting vignettes. We have chosen our material so that, we hope, the disguise of proper names and, in some instances, occupation will serve as sufficient protection. There is much current controversy about confidentiality in many spheres. Few professional or legal precedents exist for publishing verbatim sessions. Although we have done our best not to infringe on confidentiality unnecessarily, we do not harbor the illusion that it can be totally protected.

We realize that many aspects of the interaction are omitted from a transcription of an audio-recorded session. The visual and nonverbal auditory cues are absent, except for an occasional reference to a gross emotional display like laughter or weeping. While an audio or audio-visual record would certainly be more complete, such a record would not only introduce additional grave problems of confidentiality and severe practical problems of distribution, but might also overwhelm the observer with more data than he can handle. In any case, it seems to us that our transcripts of full sessions provide an adequate context for assessing what might be quite equivocal in brief segments.

We arrived at our annotations by repeated careful review of the sessions. Often we first studied a session together, then one of us annotated it, the other revised it, and finally we went over it together again. Repeated study almost invariably led to new insights and shifts of emphasis in our conclusions about underlying themes. We do not doubt that the reader will be able to add further insights. Even though we did not explicitly use the coding scheme we have developed (see Gill and Hoffman, 1982), it was clearly a guiding framework for our study of the sessions.

OVERVIEW OF THE SESSIONS

Nine sessions will be presented. Each will be separately introduced, so these remarks are to provide an overall perspective. All of the sessions are from different patients. In the nine sessions, one therapist is represented four times; one, twice; and the other four, once each. Six of the nine sessions come from the usual analytic situation, although one patient (F) was sitting up. Patients G, H, and I were being seen once a week. One reason for including the last three is that we are convinced that the principles and techniques presented in Volume I are applicable to a wide range of therapeutic settings, rather than only to the allegedly optimal one of psychoanalysis. As mentioned in Volume I, this issue is argued elsewhere (Gill, 1982). Our position on the matter accounts for our using the terms "analyst" and "therapist" interchangeably.

The particular points we intend to illustrate are stated in the annotations themselves or in our introductions or summaries. The main general points we wish to illustrate are the centrality of the patient's experience of the relationship, how this experience is alluded to in associations not manifestly about the relationship, the way in which the patient's experience of the relationship can be understood as plausible in the light of the therapeutic setting and the therapist's behavior, the usefulness of explicitly interpreting the patient's resistance to awareness of his experience of the relationship, and some of the unfortunate consequences of failing to attend to implicit indications of the patient's experience.

The first four sessions were conducted by therapists who had not been exposed to the point of view on technique we espouse while the last five were by therapists who were consciously attempting to employ our point of view. We do not mean to imply that a session must be conducted with the principles we espouse consciously in mind in order to be well done. We do believe, however, that an explicit awareness of these principles and an effort to follow them is likely to improve the quality of a therapist's work. Our primary purpose in this presentation is to illustrate the principles, both in their employment and in the failure to employ them.

The first three sessions are presented primarily to illustrate the many allusions to the patient's experience of the relationship that are not dealt with and the unfortunate consequences of the failure to deal with them. In the first, the therapist does not speak at all; in the second, the therapist speaks sparingly; and in the third, the therapist interprets fairly actively, even addressing the transference, but without taking into account the manifestly nontransference material which could have guided him to more appropriate transference interpretations. In the fourth session, the patient's experience of the relationship is interpreted, but it is the patient who brings it up rather than the therapist who searches it out. Furthermore, the analyst does not look for how his contribution to the patient's experience confirms the patient's biased expectations of human interaction.

The last five sessions demonstrate a very active examination of the patient's experience of the relationship. While they suggest the value of such work, they also show how regularly the analysis of the transference has its own repercussions on the transference — often repercussions which result in an enactment of the very patterns of interaction to which the interpretations refer.

The reader may be irritated by the exactitude with which we have reproduced what Mahl (1956) has described as speech disturbances, which make a verbatim transcript so different from the flow of written material. When such speech disturbances are heard, they are less disruptive to the sense of communication than when they are read. We decided, nevertheless, to present the original data rather than to risk distorting them by converting them into the more usual kind of edited transcripts. Incidentally this way of presenting the data may also make possible the kind of promising linguistic study reported by Dahl et al. (1978).

The reader will need to know several conventions used in presenting the transcripts. Something indecipherable is indicated by the word "inaudible" in brackets, while a question mark in brackets means the typist was not sure she had heard correctly. A silence of up to a minute is indicated by "pause," a silence of one to two minutes by "silence," and a silence of over two minutes by a specification of its length. Proper names are indicated by capital letters with the role of the person or his relationship to the patient in brackets. Names of places are handled similarly.

1

PATIENT A: SESSION 143

Introduction

We chose this session because the analyst is silent throughout
—a kind of session which the literature, our recorded material,
and discussions with colleagues lead us to believe is fairly common. We use it to illustrate the variety of useful interpretations
which would have been possible. We realize that the effects of
this analyst's silence are not necessarily generalizable to other silent hours and that the silence in this hour could be more adequately evaluated by comparing the hour with others in the
same analysis. Even so, we believe there is value in examining
this isolated session.

The Annotated Session[1]

[Patient is about five minutes late.]

P: [enters room mumbling—several inaudible words]. Really
it's terribly disappointing. [exhales] I suppose that's an example of, of not thinking well of myself, just not even trying to quit smoking because I don't think I can. And I don't
want to risk feeling guilty when I can't. I keep thinking
some day, some day, some day I'll find out what it's all
about, and just quit, and I haven't yet. I suppose that's a
digression too. I didn't come in here with anything to say
this morning, and that in itself shakes me up. [exhales]
When I don't have anything to say, I, I'm very afraid of

[1]In the original data, each line of the transcript is numbered for ease of reference.
This device has been omitted here to avoid distracting the reader.

what I'm going to say. [pause]

The hour opens with a hint of a criticism of the analyst for not helping the patient to "find out what it's all about." But then "I suppose that's a digression too" sounds as if she expects to be criticized and criticizes herself first.

P: We went to dinner at the M's Saturday night, and there was another analyst there. I think all I know are analysts and writers. And it was sort of interesting for me; it's the first time I had dealt socially with an analyst, I guess, since I started coming to you. The difference in my attitude toward one [inaudible] back in the days in which I was looking for one: I didn't drop [laughing] anything or fall off my chair or anything of that sort. Uh, he was a person. And I wasn't thinking in the back of my head, um, what kind of an analyst he would be. My husband, however, cornered him and talked to him for ages, which was sort of interesting. I don't know what about, since I was involved in another conversation, but— and I came away feeling sort of good about it, that I hadn't been shaken up; I sort of half-expected to be. But I, I somehow no longer felt—what I wanted to say was "on stage." That doesn't seem to be quite right—but as if I were being x-rayed. I guess "x-ray" is more accurate. [pause] Uh, I don't have the slightest idea whether that's really worthy of remark or not; it struck me as being interesting, but that's because it concerned me.

Again she hints at what could be a criticism of the analyst, namely, that he scrutinizes her with an impersonal, clinical eye, but she quickly turns to criticizing herself, implying she does not know whether she is satisfying the analyst's criteria for useful associating.

P: And because my attitude toward you and toward the, the other [sigh] psychiatrists I'd met in the preceding year struck me as being so peculiar, I suppose I felt as if this was some sort of step forward, to feel reasonably self-confident, to the point where you, you didn't feel shaken up. Of course

I suppose I'm no longer looking, so that's, that's a factor. [sigh] I suppose, come to think of it, that my attitude toward you, particularly, and the other two, only, only kind of peripherally, because I sort of took an instant dislike to them both, was very similar to the, the attitude I had toward priests as a kid. I was always very uncomfortable being in a room with one, as if he knew what was going on in the deep dirty depths of my soul. As if, uh, his presence was an accusation [exhales] — the eye of God, or something. This seems very wandering. [pause]

If there was any question that her earlier references to the other analyst at the party implied something about her experience of the analytic relationship, it is dispelled now. And once again, she stops to criticize her associations.

P: He told a, a sort of a comic story about an incident with a patient which I'm, I'm, I don't think is exactly off the subject·because it illustrates a feeling I've felt in here.

She explicitly relates her feelings there and here and apologizes yet again.

P: She was telling him about a dream, and all of a sudden she said, "I smell something burning." And, uh, come to think of it, it may even be an apocryphal story. It sounds sort of like it now that I tell it — an analyst's story. And he thought, "My, how interesting," and was trying to follow this down in the dream, and all of a sudden realized that his wastebasket was on fire. And he went dashing madly into the john to put it out, and came back and sat down in his chair. And she said, perfectly serenely, "Now, about this dream. . ." Um, and he said, "Of course, I didn't let her go on; I pulled back to discussing the wastebasket. But how marvelously well-trained she was." And I thought that that's exactly what kind of position you're in here, all the time. If she hadn't gone on with the dream, if she had started talking about the wastebasket, then why wasn't she talking about the dream? It seems very unfair, as if you just absolutely can't win. Of course you would say that my purpose is not to win, and using that phrase is an indication of how mixed up I've got things, and I expect you're right. But no matter in what direction you go, somehow it's, it's a resistance against something. [pause] And that may be one of the reasons why when I don't have anything very specific to say, I fear to say anything.

The sarcastic criticism of the analyst in the story seems clear. He is so wrapped up in silently following an intrapsychic puzzle (he thought, not he said, "how interesting") that he is oblivious to practical reality. After he finally does deal with the reality of the fire, he notes with amusement that the patient wanted to continue to associate to her dream as though nothing had happened. He regards her as "marvelously well-trained."

The patient begins to criticize the present analyst, clearly saying she feels in a no-win situation with him. However, she answers for him and finds the fault within herself. The analyst could interpret her apparent inability to let a criticism of him stand. He could pursue further her experience of the relationship—for example, by asking whether she feels he is trying to train her, by asking whether she feels he will turn any criticism of himself back on her, or by inquiring about other ways the story may allude to the analytic relationship. But he says nothing.

P: I had a dream last Tuesday afternoon when— after the squabble I got into here with you, which I meant to bring up on Friday and sort of didn't get around to. My dreams keep getting more and more realistic. I was in a session with you, and I was talking about a dream. And in the dream I had been a mouse, which is fairly easy to run down because that's what you called me on Tuesday. There was something about the dream that was terribly, terribly important that I couldn't remember—this is the dream within a dream. And you were very angry at me, because I was, I was hiding this recollection. And in the dream I wasn't hiding it, I simply couldn't remember it, that is, I wasn't consciously hiding it. And I was just desperate, because you were so angry. I was frantic to remember it. And then I just suddenly did, and what I remembered was that the cheese [laughing] I was eating didn't taste very good. Then I woke up, terribly pleased that I'd remembered this deeply significant thing. And when I woke up of course it didn't seem very significant, or at least its significance did not leap to the eye. And I've been puzzling over it ever since, and I have about a zillion associations, none of which seem to get anywhere. [sigh]

So she has been in a squabble with the analyst and he has called her a mouse. Indeed, with her continual apologies, she seems to be behaving like one. The manifest content of the dream bears a similarity to her associations up to now. She is attempting to please the critical analyst who blames her unfairly. She also cannot tell whether what she is thinking is significant or not. She has been attempting to understand the dream as though that were her job. Apparently, she feels she cannot look to the analyst for help with it.

P: It's like other dreams I've had when I've suddenly known the answer to what I was looking for, and when I wake up I can't remember what the answer was, or the answer seems so buried in symbolism that I, I despair of ever getting at it. If indeed it's the answer, that's I suppose another question. I, I was sort of an odd, stick-figure, cartoon kind of mouse, with a, um, a stick body, just legs and, and arms with kind of funny stick fingers, but sort of a big Walt Disney mouse kind of head, big ears, whiskers. And what it reminded me of were cartoons I had seen as a kid, a very small kid. We had a movie projector and a few cartoons and my father used to run them for me occasionally. This was when I was, oh, maybe three. I just loved them. Although I didn't like regular movies at all, I, my mother took me to a couple of them and I was very frightened, because the picture was so big. But these were of course smaller. And the, and the other thing I remembered was Archie and Mehitabel, but then it struck me that thinking about these things, in neither one of them were, were there any mice, 'cause Archie was a cockroach. And in the one of these cartoons I remembered, the, the creature that was being chased was not a mouse but a bird, a sort of parrot-like bird. And, and the correlation between those two is the presence of a cat, which I suppose goes back to the, the cats of my childhood. In this cartoon, I, I don't remember the, most of it very well [analyst coughs], but I remember the last frame extremely well because it was very puzzling to me as a kid. There was a, an empty birdcage, the door was open, and there was a sign on it that said: "to let." And I only realized that much much later. I think one time, or, or a couple of times maybe after my father got home from the war, we dug out the projector and showed the films, which by that time were falling apart. But when I was very small I thought what it said was "toilet" [laughing], which strikes me as, as being interesting from one standpoint and that is that I sort of knew how to read at the age of three, which I hadn't realized before. It was absolutely baffling to me, why this birdcage should be labeled a toilet. And yet apparently I never asked anybody what it meant, and when I saw the film a number of years later and realized that it said: "to let," not "toilet," I didn't know what that meant. It was a British cartoon apparently. And, and I did at that point ask my mother what "to let" meant, and she said it meant "for rent." [pause] [sigh] I don't exactly know where that goes. My subconscious is a toilet? Which I dare say I think it is, but— you seem very restive this morning. Does that mean this is terribly significant, or terribly dull? [exhales] I shall have to find out for myself apparently.

Direct references to the analytic situation cease and she begins to talk about her childhood. She tells of a misunderstanding, concerning which for a long time she did not ask for enlightenment. Perhaps here, too, there is something she does not understand which could be cleared up if she could bring herself to ask.

Then she returns to the analytic situation and asks a direct question, the same one she has been asking in one way or another all along: Is she saying anything useful or not? Now the question is more clearly whether she is boring the analyst. She gets no answer and concludes that she will have to depend on herself for any enlightenment. It seems likely, then, that the stories she is telling are primarily designed to interest the analyst, that is, to gain his approval. Even her attempt at interpretation (i.e., wondering whether her "subconscious" is a toilet) appears to be designed to comply with his expectations. In this instance, as in many others, her compliance is not without a tone of annoyance and sarcasm. The compliance itself and the resentment about the role she feels forced to play both beg for an empathic interpretation from the analyst.

P: It certainly reminds me again of both the cat-bathing incident — goddammit, I can't remember the word. "Enema." I blacked out that word totally, I couldn't remember it — and the enema incident, which apparently I don't want to remember. Because it seems to me they took place in the same bathroom. But other than that I've never been able to see the connection, unless I thought somehow that the enema was a punishment for bathing the cat, or the cat was taken away from me because I made such a fuss about the enema. You know, it is true that my pets were consistently taken away from me. The bird was, the cat was, the rabbit was. And my sister's cat killed my turtle and one of my goldfish. I, I really never — at least the, the two smaller, the incidents that occurred when I was smaller — the bird and the cat — I never did understand. It seemed to me a, a question of convenience; the rabbit I understood, because I was going to camp, and my mother just didn't want to be bothered taking care of a rabbit over the summer. Also I expect they were going away for awhile. But the bird, which we had when I was very small, under three, was given to my grandmother. I don't know why. And he died. And the cat was left in R [place] at the end of one summer, ostensibly because he was hiding in the furnace room, and my mother just didn't feel like crawling around on pipes and fishing him out. And also maybe she felt a little guilty. I suppose she thought that he was very happy there and he would be miserable back in the apartment, which was no doubt quite true. But I was very unhappy about that; it seemed, uh, wrong. He was my cat, or so it had been proclaimed. I told you, didn't I, the last time we were talking about him, that he was supposed to be a girl and he turned out to be a boy? I think I did. I had even given him a girl's name, then we took him to the vet and it was disclosed that it was a boy, so we had to change his name. And I remember quite clearly my mother asking upon that occasion how soon we could have him castrated. Charming story. And I asked her what that meant, and she explained it to me, and I didn't quite understand why that was necessary. [sigh] [pause] There's something about that cat, I guess, but I [sigh], I don't know exactly what. There are, I suppose, about 15 things about that cat and I don't know which is important and which isn't or what it all means.

The patient's sense of puzzlement at her parents' behavior and her feeling that she was treated unfairly by them seem to parallel her experience of the immediate interaction with the analyst. He, too, she must feel, leaves her to divine by herself the reasons for the deprivations she is called upon to endure. In the current situation, she again tries to rationalize his silence by reference to the possibility that there is something wrong with her associations: they may lack significance. Of course, she is also implicitly complaining about his failure to help her establish where the significance lies. One could also speculate that she identifies herself with the cat which the mother (analyst) doesn't want to crawl around on pipes to fish out (rescue from her perplexity by an intervention).

P: I gave him a bath and felt terribly guilty about it, because I had been warned not to, and I'd been warned that he'd be very unhappy about it, and indeed he was. I have a very clear picture of myself sitting huddled in a corner of the bathroom, with the cat wrapped in a towel, trying to dry him off and apologizing to him and crying and telling him I was sorry. I was very upset. [pause] And that was certainly a source of guilt, and I may [exhales] have felt that giving him to my grandmother was a punishment for me —

"See, you don't do right by your cat, we'll give him to somebody who will." Except that oddly enough I don't think my mother even knew that I'd given him a bath. I certainly don't remember being punished for it or being talked to about it. I may successfully have, have hidden the fact, by drying him off and letting him go. And maybe that was even worse; maybe if I had been punished for it I wouldn't have felt so bad about it. I don't remember wanting to be mean to him particularly; it was — if I have a memory of what my motives were — it, they were kind of experimental. In a way it was almost a "don't put beans up your nose" sort of thing, uh — don't give the cat a bath. Well, instantly, then [laughing], I want to give the cat a bath to see what will happen. I don't think, for instance, that I was trying to drown him. If, if I was, I've certainly successfully hidden that from myself. But I don't know. If he was supposed to be a girl and he turned out to be a boy, maybe I did want to drown him. [pause] I don't think I did, though. Wouldn't I have some sort of, I don't know, niggling memory, if I did — some hint of motive? [pause] Well, I don't know whether I would or not. It seems to me I would. [exhales]

She seems to be holding a conversation with herself in lieu of any response from the analyst. The tone grows desperate as she searches for something he will find worthy of comment.

P: And he was so beautiful. He was, I expect, the prettiest cat I've ever seen. He was huge, and coal black — not a bit of white on him anywhere — long silky hair. I suppose he wasn't really so big; he seemed big to me because I was small. He seemed about twice as big as any cat we have right now. But whenever I see a black cat — this may be the Halloween influence, I don't know — I feel immediately much warmer toward it than toward any other cat. Bought a pumpkin yesterday at a place in Y and they had a black cat and I wanted very much to touch him. He didn't want to be touched. And when we got married, we acquired two of them right after settling down into our apartment, and they have since died. That was sort of a deliberate attempt somehow to repeat— we, we went to the animal shelter to pick out a cat, and they had two black cats, and it had not been our intention to get two, but when I saw two I wanted two. I didn't want just one. I, I couldn't have picked which one I wanted. And so we took them both. And one of them was, I suppose, the nicest cat we've ever known in terms of temperament. He was also the most accident-prone cat. Nothing but disasters from the day we acquired him. He came down with distemper three days after we had him, which left his rear legs permanently crippled, and he walked very strangely. He had no control over his rear end at all, so when he ran it would wiggle back and forth like that. And he finally died a couple of years ago of skin cancer; it was horrible. Just wasn't a thing the doctor could do. And he was, oh, he was so pathetic. He knew how awful he looked and he used to hide all the time because my daughter and her friends made fun of him. And we finally had him put to sleep. [sigh] But in between the distemper and the skin cancer there were kidney ailments, and he got hit by a car [sigh], fell off the sea wall into the lagoon and almost drowned. Poor fellow. His brother was a neurotic mess. He was a fraidy cat. You came near him and he jumped up and ran and hid. But he was beautiful; absolutely gorgeous cat. Nothing ever happened to him, except he came home at five o'clock one morning covered with kerosene once, I think [inaudible]. Somebody had apparently doused him in kerosene with the intent of putting him on, uh, fire. I can't think why else he would have done it. We had to give him a bath, come to think of it. My husband did that, because the vet said the kerosene was poisonous and he would lick it off and poison himself if we didn't, so we scrubbed him with detergent. And I suppose that was a repetition of that incident for me. Boy, was he mad. He went round and round the bathroom like a, like a racing car in one of those round turns, just, he went around [chuckle] the walls, never touching the floor, peeing madly as he went. What a scene!

She seems to be trying to entertain the analyst with her stories.

At the same time she attempts to do analytic "work"—"I suppose that was a repetition of that incident"—but he stands firm.

P: The ASPCA killed him. We'd taken him to their hospital on N Street or wherever it is, it was near where we lived then, also for a kidney ailment. And they could have saved him if they had operated on him fast enough, but they didn't. They fooled around for a couple of days and he died. And one of their receptionists called to tell me, and announced in this sort of sepulchral voice that the cat had died; it was somehow comic. I, it was sad. I was sorry that he had died, and I was mad at them, but her tone and voice were somehow comic. And she asked me if I would like the corpse, and I, I thought "Christ [laughing], what on earth would I do with a dead cat in a four-bedroom railroad flat in Z [town]?" We didn't have a yard. There was just a slab of cement out back. I should go down and dig up cement so I could bury the cat. Or maybe sneak into V Park at night and bury him there. And she finally assured me that they would dispose of him. [exhales] I should have asked for him back and taken him to have an autopsy done on him so I could prove that they'd killed him, the bastards. I hate the ASPCA. We were going to sue them a couple of weeks ago, but the ACLU wouldn't take our case. Since you have a dog [sound of lighter] you may know that dog license money in the city of T goes to the ASPCA instead of the city, and J [husband] and I believe that's wrong. [pause] [exhales] That is a digression, unquestionably.

The cat died because they fooled around instead of operating. The latent meaning may be that the analyst's silence is doing nothing and the analysis may die. She may be growing increasingly angry at his inactivity. Perhaps malpractice would warrant suing him. But this covert denouncement is followed by overt self-criticism. She is the one who is wasting time with her digression.

P: And now we have just cats, and I'm fond of them all, but they're just cats. When I am very rich I'm going to get a pair of Burmese cats, and breed them, and it's going to satisfy my instincts for having kittens around the house without giving me the problem of what the hell you do with the kittens when they're eight weeks old. Because Burmese cats are very desirable and you can sell them for lots of money to people who will take extremely good care of them. [pause] [exhales] My daughter came home from school a couple of weeks ago and announced that one of her teachers had to give away a rabbit and could she have it. And although I'd declared a moratorium on pets some months ago, I had no problem with this rabbit at all. And I'm sure it was because I had one as a kid and somehow felt that whatever I had as a kid she ought to be entitled to. And by golly this one wasn't going to end up at the ASPCA because she went to camp in the summer. [sigh] [exhales] And so now we have a rabbit too. [pause]

She will take better care of her daughter than she was taken care of. A model for the analyst?

P: You know who gave me that rabbit? That fellow with the red hair, and the restoration colony name — X [inaudible]. Maybe that's why my father was so angry about it. It was at Easter time, and my father brought home a cardboard box one night after work, and said, "Here's a present for you, from X." I had no notion that there was anything alive in the box at all; I thought it was, you know, maybe a stuffed rabbit, or, I didn't know what, but it just never occurred to me it was alive. And I started to open the box and I, I heard some scratching and so I, and I suddenly knew that it was something alive, but even at that point I thought maybe it was baby chicks, or baby ducks, or something. And I was just astonished to get a rabbit, and delighted; it was wonderful, I was so pleased. That may be one of the nicest presents I've ever had in my life. He wasn't even a very special rabbit. My daughter's rabbit is gorgeous — he's huge and all white, with the requisite pink eyes — but this one was just a, a spotted-rabbit-type rabbit of no consequence. Except that I was very fond of him. I used to take him to bed with me at night, which was my mother's despair, because then he would end up with rabbit marbles all over the bed. Oh, I didn't mind. And he chewed a pair of sandals of mine to bits, which also upset her, and I didn't mind that either. [pause] And I had to. . . [series of inaudible words] [voice softens] The fight I had with my father about it—well, I guess it wasn't exactly a fight, I just got slapped. I suppose that's, that's one of the clearest memories I have of, of the kind of anger that seems to me so characteristic of him, although I do think that's the only memory I have of, of him ever punishing me physically, except for the spanking incident, which was different because [inaudible] that wasn't done in anger, that was kind of *pro forma*. But this was just a seething fury, over something that was so unreasonable [sigh] and, in its way, so surprising. I, I suppose you would argue that it wasn't surprising since I had deliberately defied him, but the magnitude of it was surprising to me. I would have expected him to be annoyed or maybe even angry, but I would never have expected this towering, massive anger, and his striking me.

Again, she supplies the analyst's part of an imagined conversation, and, as usual, it puts her in the wrong. Is there a reference here to the "squabble" with the analyst? It is quite possible that his silence is experienced as towering, unreasonable anger. But for what infraction? The squabble last time? Or is it that she is failing to associate properly and, hence, resisting or "defying" the analyst now.

P: It's cold in here [sigh], and I don't know why I noticed that just now, but it is. I'm cold. I suppose it was cold out there on the porch that night, because it was—terrific thunderstorm. That's why I was so worried about him, because it was cold and raining so hard. And I was afraid the thunder and lightning was frightening him. There's some sort of relationship between the magnitude of my father's anger and the magnitude of that storm, I think—nature overdoing it

on all counts. [pause] I did deliberately defy him, no question about it, but I didn't do it with the idea of getting
caught; it wasn't the, the same thing as the hand-washing
thing. I didn't expect to be discovered with the rabbit, and
I suppose that added to my surprise. I snuck out there to
see if the rabbit was all right. [pause] I wonder if I ever will
get that one settled. [pause]

Will I ever learn anything in here? The cold may be a metaphor
for the atmosphere of the analysis. She is concerned about the
welfare of a helpless creature, but she cannot expect the same
kind of concern for herself.

P: I, I don't know whether I've ever talked about this incident
     before—but, for some reason it, it comes to mind in line
     with this. I'm not quite sure why—a totally different inci-
     dent. I think, come to think of it, it even happened at a
     much later time. But I suppose it, it illustrates to me the
     fact that I just never knew what my parents' reaction to
     something was going to be. My mother had fixed ham and
     eggs, on a, a Haviland platter, which she liked very much.
     And she told me to take it into the dining room and put it
     on the table, and also I'm sure warned me to be careful.
     And [chuckle] I suppose because she had warned me to be
     careful, I wasn't, and I tripped and fell and dropped the
     platter. And it was, oh God, what a mess—fried eggs in
     every direction. And this beautiful platter, which she lov-
     ed, broken. And if I had ever done anything for which I
     expected practically to be sent to jail, I suppose that would
     have been it, because the whole thing was clearly my fault,
     and I had ruined our dinner, made a God-awful mess, and
     broken her favorite platter in the bargain. And nobody was
     mad at me. My father was there, and I would have ex-
     pected him to just raise absolute hell because he was always
     after me for being clumsy. [sigh] And it struck everybody
     as being somewhat comic, somehow. I mean, the mess was
     just so awful that it was ludicrous. And we ended up clean-
     ing it up and going out to dinner, which was sort of a treat,
     you know. I, I don't know why they're related in my mind

exactly, except they both happened in the kitchen and were concerned with, with dinner and so forth. The rabbit being concerned with dinner because I had snuck out to see him when I was carrying plates back from the dining room into the kitchen, which was my job, one of my jobs. [pause]

Her primary feeling is puzzlement: she was scolded unreasonably, on the one hand, and not scolded when she fully expected to be, on the other. She does not understand how the analyst is responding to her. She continues to try to be a good patient. She tries to decipher the meaning of the sequence of her associations — "for some reason it comes to mind in line with this" — presumably the analyst's job. But she does not know what he wants.

P: How about saying something at this point, like: "Wow, this is significant," or "Wow, this is totally insignificant, talk about something else." [pause]

Her sense of frustration and anger surface in this strikingly direct appeal for a response. The pause itself shows that she is not merely "associating"; she stops and waits for him to speak. He remains ostensibly impervious, however, and she retreats, in what follows, to her usual effort to take him off the hook by answering her own question.

P: I suppose it is significant in that it illustrates that I felt myself to be in a situation in which you couldn't count on anything, you couldn't even count on what things drove people up the wall, and what things didn't. I'm perfectly confident that on other occasions I might either have gone to see the rabbit and not invoked anybody's anger, or dropped the same platter and been punished for weeks for it. [pause] And yet at the same time I, I feel somehow guilty about even criticizing my parents for being inconsistent because everybody's inconsistent. [sigh] And I am sure that there are things that my daughter does that upset me at one time and don't at others.

Now she summarizes the theme herself: she couldn't make sense of how she was treated and yet feels she shouldn't criticize her parents. Can one doubt that her feelings about the analyst are similar?

A: We'll stop for now. [clears throat] And tomorrow, I, I'd like to try to meet around 9:20.
P: 9:20. OK.
A: Yeah. I may be a few minutes late, but I'll be here before 9:30.
P: OK.

ADDITIONAL COMMENTS

It is sometimes argued that the analyst's silence is desirable because it permits the transference to grow in intensity and clarity. Does it do so here? With regard to the issue of intensity, consider first the patient's explicit references to the relationship. Remarks to the effect that the analyst gives her no clue as to whether he is satisfied with her associations are scattered throughout. Her outright appeal for a comment near the end is especially clear, but the wish has been evident all along. Occasionally she attributes a remark to the analyst in an imaginary conversation. Although the remark seems invariably critical of her, she never explicitly says so. Criticism of the therapist is most explicit early in the session, in the statement that the analytic situation is unfair. It never again returns in so clear a form.

As for implicit references to the relationship, one can infer from various associations that the patient is critical of the analyst, although this inference is most plausible in the early rather than the late material, especially in her opening associations about the other analyst. In fact the patient herself draws a connection between these associations and her experience of the analytic relationship. Possible implied criticism of the analyst is invariably followed by self-criticism, but again this sequence is not made explicit.

The patient's frustration does seem to become more intense. But the change is not merely quantitative; it is qualitative as well. By the end of the session, the length of the analyst's silence is the source of a particular kind of frustration, which could not have been the case, by definition, at the beginning of the hour. This, perhaps, is where the issue is really joined. If the intent is to provide an atmosphere of "optimal frustration" so that a pre-formed transference will grow in intensity over time, keeping silent becomes an effective strategy to bring about such a strictly quantitative variation. If, however, one views the transference as a fluid aspect of the patient's experience, the nuances of which change as a function, in part, of the nature of the analyst's behavior, one is obviously more inclined to advocate interpreting these various nuances as they become prominent from moment to moment throughout the session. (Incidentally, the manipulative use of silence is an example of how the quantitative aspect of the economic point of view of metapsychology can influence technique. The current controversy between metapsychology and hermeneutics as an overall framework for psychoanalysis would benefit from detailed explication of the ways in which metapsychological considerations underlie technical practices [Apfelbaum, 1965; Gill, 1976].)

Silence is not inactivity on the analyst's part. In fact, as it continues, it does not simply add to the patient's conviction about its meaning. Instead, as noted above, it promotes new constructions that represent attempts to make sense of its duration. In the session presented here, the patient may initially feel that the silence is consistent with her view that the analysis is unfair because whatever she says is wrong. But by the end of the hour, she may well feel not only that the analysis is unfair but also that the silence reflects an obstinate or even angry refusal by the analyst to offer her anything.

Another argument for maintaining silence is that it permits the patient's associations to develop without interference. In this session, there is a lot of childhood material about puzzlement at being treated unfairly and insensitively, but this material can also readily be understood as a reaction to the silence itself. In its style, the patient's reaction seems to be a continuing effort to entertain and interest the analyst. The content, dealing as it does with being treated unfairly and insensitively, may be a disguised elaboration of the sporadic, though brief, explicit expressions of distress about the analyst's silence. Although some inferences about how the patient experiences the silence are fairly clear, we can only guess at the changing meanings to the patient of the analyst's silence because she is not helped to overcome her resistance to expressing her feelings about it more directly. Her inability to speak freely is enhanced by her uncertainty about what the analyst wants to hear.

Our annotations obviously indicate that we believe the analyst could have intervened more usefully. These suggestions for interventions have to be evaluated in the light of the fact that any intervention might well have changed the course of the hour. Nevertheless, it seems worthwhile to show what could have been said at any given point, assuming nothing had been said up to that time.

The patient's experience of the relationship might well have been further clarified. One way would have been to refer explicitly to her apparent difficulty in criticizing the analyst and her belief that he is critical of her. Another would have been to pursue the allusions suggested in the material not manifestly about the transference. The comparison between the analyst and the priest presented a golden opportunity for such an approach. Other examples include the possibility that she feels that the analyst, like the one in the story, is missing a real fire under his nose while he is pursuing some exotic fantasy, or that he, too, would appreciate a "marvelously well-trained" patient. Still other inferences might have been drawn from the childhood material—for example, that the analyst, like her parents, is insensitive to her needs, or quite plausibly, that he is unpredictable and that his silence may signify an enraged reaction to a minor provocation.

Another potential line of inquiry, as was emphasized in Volume I, would be to look at the aspects of the analyst's behavior which, from the patient's viewpoint, seem to justify the various conclusions she has drawn. Specifically, for example, how has the analyst led her to believe that whatever she says, he will say she should have been talking about something else?

The patient is asking for help. One could argue that to give her help is to manipulate the transference. But our suggestion is not merely to give help, but to examine the meaning of her asking for it, which means examining her experience of the relationship—what bases she has for her view that the analytic situation is unfair, why she feels the analyst is critical of her, why she seems so cautious about criticizing the analyst, why it is so important to her to know whether he finds her productions satisfactory, and so forth. It is possible that such an investigation would lead the analyst to a new recognition of how some of his behavior is experienced. It might even lead him to change his behavior. That would not mean that he was attempting to manipulate the transference, whereas before he had been "neutral." It would mean, rather, that he was influencing the patient's experience of the relationship in a different way. And if he did change his behavior, he would need to continue to examine how the patient experienced *that*.

2

PATIENT B: SESSION 119

In this session the analyst is again relatively silent, though not entirely so, as in the previous session. As we shall see, in this case, a fleeting explicit reference to the relationship at the begining, a recent experience, and a dream could have been integrated to yield an important insight into the patient's experience of the relationship. What happens instead is that the issue is enacted, rather than explored and understood, by the participants.

The Annotated Session

P: [four-minute silence] I was just about, um, well—two different things in a way—um, my comparing how I felt yesterday to today. And then it just seemed to parallel having to actually start by saying something here—that there were lots of things going through my mind while I was, after I came in. But just to begin, no matter what it was I began with, I was finding very hard, just to say the first word, and it was the same thing as yesterday. I had thought about going shopping and I, I couldn't get myself to make the first step outside and, and to go to a store. I just somehow felt as if I couldn't do it and I found lots of excuses not to. And then today I just did, and then it was fine and I, and it didn't bother me and I could make decisions and choices. But I guess that was part of it yesterday—I just didn't feel I could make the decisions that I'd

29

> have to make. Which leads me to wonder: Is there something that I don't want to say, and that's why it was hard to start? I was — maybe this is it, I don't know — I was thinking of [clears throat] sort of a double reaction I had when I saw the way you were standing holding the door, because my first inclination was you were sort of "Oh Lord, here we go again" inside, and, and impatient. And then, and then immediately I started thinking, "Well, how could you stand while you're waiting holding the door and what does it matter?" And it— I, I think I'm sort of torn between the two attitudes, but it isn't bothering me the way some days it would completely crush me if I started thinking the way I did at first. I wouldn't get beyond the way I felt at first. For instance, I think if yesterday I'd seen you standing that way and I'd had that initial reaction, that's what I would have thought. [cough] [pause]

The analyst might have done well to ask for further elaboration of this very vivid experience of a nonverbal interaction at the beginning of the hour. He could inquire, for example, about what the patient thinks is the reason for the analyst's alleged impatience. What, after all, does she mean when she attributes the thought to him: "Oh Lord, here we go again"? Moreover, it's likely that there is a relationship between this experience at the door and the four-minute silence that ensues. By saying nothing, the analyst risks wasting an opportunity to engage the patient in an explication of an immediate and very charged experience. If he chooses to remain silent, as he does, he should certainly listen for and interpret subsequent associations in light of the themes that have been introduced so strikingly right at the beginning.

P: I was also thinking when I did get out today, that it, um, I think I've al —, I've said this in other ways, but I think one reason that I have in the past wanted to have children or a child is because, well, it would sort of give me a direction. There are certain things you'd have to do to care for the child, and aside from wanting to have something dependent on me and so forth, I think just the fact that I'd be focusing on something is part of it. Then I would get out, because want — , wanting to get your child out and there'd be no other decisions than that. Maybe where you'd go to. But, but then I, then one of the things that I think I'm still afraid of is that the confusion and the pressures on me would increase in a way and the— it would be different types of decisions, but there still would be those that would have to be made and there'll be new ones that I'm not used to, and that I think frightens me. [silence]

After the four-minute silence, the patient acknowledges that she has trouble getting started—in the hour and elsewhere—and that she thought the analyst anticipated the hour with impatience. Perhaps she feels his impatience has to do with her inertia. Then she says she wants a child to give her direction. It seems reasonable to conclude that these themes are connected. Perhaps she feels the analyst is impatient with her for being unable to start without being directed.

P: And another thing—I don't know how much this has to do with it—I, I think it's more the attitude I somehow began the day with—but I had my hair done this morning and I finally got around to saying to my hairdresser that I wanted my hair to be done differently. And at that point I wasn't too sure exactly what I wanted and I was still hesitant anyway to direct him too much since I was unsure. But yet I was still willing to try something different. And what he did I didn't like. And I sort of half-changed it, but I still, I don't know, it didn't bother me. It was sort of: If you don't try then you can't know. And I know that, I knew that other people didn't think it looked as well as other styles on me, but that didn't really seem to bother me that much either. And I, I don't know, I just somehow felt a little bit freer, again as if: What does it matter because I've gotten that much closer to know what I do want? But then I think of something that happened this weekend which— the closer I get to know what I do want, the more I sort of reject it. Um, we saw the movie *I Am Curious Yellow* and I think that I was aroused or something by the fact that there

was a nude man in the film. And in any case I felt that I
wanted to have intercourse with F [husband] and I felt
much more intimate with him, much more interested in
this type of thing. But then when it came right down to it,
I, I was more inhibited than I'd been in a long time, as if I
felt very guilty that I was admitting that I felt this way.

The theme of a struggle between wanting to be directed and
taking initiative continues. She directed the hairdresser somewhat and was pleased to feel freer. She even felt like taking the
initiative sexually with her husband, but then began feeling
guilty and inhibited. The analyst should be alert to how this
conflict finds expression in the patient's relationship with him.
The patient's difficulty starting at the beginning of the hour may
well be associated with a conflict paralleling the one with her
husband. Also, although this is certainly speculative, it is possible that the patient's vivid impression of the analyst standing at
the door may have been sexually arousing and may have something to do either with her own "inhibitions" at the beginning of
the session or with what she perceives as his, or both.

A: Do you remember what you actually thought about at the
    time?
P: Which time? The movie or . . .?
A: Well, either, but particularly the one you felt inhibited.
P: Yeah. Well, it was— I wanted him to, um, have an or-
    gasm. I wanted to, well actually I wanted to just mastur-
    bate him because I didn't want to be involved. And it, and
    I felt very, almost sickened if I began to respond, but it
    gave me some pleasure for him to respond. And yet, it was
    that mixed thing of: I couldn't respond without feeling
    sickened by it and yet, um, I felt very definitely the lack,
    that I wasn't responding. And it was funny, just, um—I
    don't know whether there's any connection or if the con-
    nection is more, um, with the mixed feelings I've had
    about the dream and I had concerning the instructor and
    my other reactions. Um, but I think it was Saturday night.

She vividly describes a conflict about responding sexually, as though she attempted to resolve the anxiety about sexual initiative by remaining uninvolved. She refers to a dream which has been discussed earlier about an instructor, a likely figure to represent an analyst (although we are not told whether this connection was considered). It's probably wise for the analyst to await further developments, especially as they may refer to himself, whether directly or by allusion. Nevertheless, a plausible speculation is that she is expressing an identification with the analyst, whom she perceives as wanting to remain uninvolved.

P: We saw the movie Saturday night and then Saturday night I had a dream that, um, was in a class situation. And I don't remember if there was anybody in particular who was running the class, but it was something we did do in a, in a way in the class I'm taking; because we were all, we'd all made puppets. And the part I recall now about the dream was my playing around with the puppet I made and feeling fairly free and yet always knowing that pretty soon I'd be asked to perform in front of others. And when this did happen in the dream and I had to make my puppet work in front of others, I completely lost control over it. I, I just sort of froze and I couldn't do anything.

The dream includes several possible allusions to the analysis. The class may represent the analytic situation and the manipulation of puppets suggests a continuation of the theme of who directs whom. That she froze when she had to perform sounds very much like her freezing in the sexual situation, and may also allude to freezing up with the analyst, as she does, perhaps, at the beginning of the hour. There is a rather neat parallel between feeling free when she is by herself playing around with the puppet but then freezing once the performance begins and her description of the contrast between anticipating a session and actually beginning. Anticipating the hour, rehearsing for it, as it were, many things go through her mind, but once the session begins she has trouble saying the first word (p. 29).

The reference to performing in front of others may also allude to the fact that the analysis is being recorded. With that possibility in mind, one might wonder whether the one who freezes represents not only the patient but perhaps the analyst too. As for the specific content, given that the patient has already referred to wanting to masturbate her husband, the reference to performing with a hand puppet makes it inevitable that an analyst will think masturbation is being alluded to in some way.

P: And then I think there was some awareness again of, um —because I had frozen and I wasn't handling my puppet, especially after having practiced much better or playedwith it beforehand—again of incurring disapproval. And in fact, there is a definite connection—because —with what was happening with F—because I think what I did with my puppet when I realized I was freezing and was going to get disapproval anyway since I wasn't going to be able to perform with it, I then—I can't remember now exactly how I did this—but in some way I turned it back on the class and asked them to tell them, tell my puppet about themselves. And somehow it ended up I and my puppet weren't doing anything and that I was making the class do it. And even though it was still a fiasco, somebody else was acting, it wasn't me. Somebody else was doing the work or, or expressing themselves, revealing themselves. And that is what I was doing with F. And it was that inability to feel free to really express myself and know what I liked and didn't like that I think was what was bothering me in that class. When I felt his disapproval, even if he really didn't give it, I assumed he was, because I knew I wasn't doing something that is a standard of his and that I wanted to be able to meet. [pause]

She is aware of a connection between the episode with her husband and the dream. She dealt with the situation in the dream by getting someone else to act and she dealt with the situation with her husband by trying to get him to act.

The theme of self-revelation may be another allusion to the analysis. Perhaps the patient represents the analyst via identification when she reports dealing with her own paralysis by "making the class do it." In other words, she may have the idea that the analyst feels inadequate so he throws all the responsibility for the analytic work onto her. Some support for this hypothesis can be found in the several pauses and silences that have punctuated the session so far, in addition to the four-minute silence at the beginning.

It is not clear whose disapproval she fears. She may mean her husband and she may mean the instructor in the earlier dream. But the most explicit reference so far to a disapproving figure whose standards she may not be meeting is to the analyst, whom she experiences as impatient.

P: And its interesting that it's so— the dream which had— I know I was very emotionally involved in this because Sunday morning when I did, I was sort of— I always had the feeling I was kind of half-awake when I was having the dream since I do remember some of it. And then later I just had this feeling that my mind was just full of things and I didn't know exactly what they were. And we, um, went for a drive. We were going hiking and had to drive quite a way and I just wanted to be quiet and say nothing and just think; try to get to what all these things were.

This may also imply an identification with the silent analyst, who is trying to figure all this out.

P: And the first thing that I began to think of—and after this I recalled the dream again—was that, well, two aspects that I think are, are involved in why I find it so hard to make decisions and know what I want, to even have the confidence to think what I like and don't like and want and don't want. Because, first of all, in our family we weren't ever asked in anything that really mattered: "What do you think?" or "What do you want?" That I can recall. And even if we were, still my parents made it very clear that their opinions were the ones we should have and that if we didn't agree then we just were stupid and didn't know anything, and, or immature, and when we grew up we'd understand. And then the other thing is—I think is perhaps even more important—is just the way my father is when you do agree with him, when you choose the same foods or agree on political philosophy or anything. That it's almost like you're a comrade. You— there's a closeness and he's very moved by this because, well, in a way it's giving him his confidence, I suppose, that he needs. But even, just like ordering an ice cream cone at a Howard Johnson's or something. If you chose the same flavor as he did, then there was somehow an intimacy between you and he'd get in a very good mood. And I don't know, you got his approval and, and in a way his affection by choosing as he chose. And I th——, I don't know, I was thinking, too, in terms of how so often I'm ask——, I want F to make his decision first because now I think I'm doing this with F—that if we both are eating the same thing or somehow share the same opinion, there's a certain intimacy or closeness. [pause] And on the other hand, that this would lead me to assume that if you strike out on your own, have your own ideas or choose your own kinds of choices, you get disapproval. And I know this is true in, in discussing political things with my parents that this would happen. And I was just, it just occurred to me now that in my family when we were little, everybody liked ice cream but me. And I really didn't like it and, and I only enjoyed one or two flavors. [cough] And it was sort of like I was a family outcast because I didn't enjoy ice cream as everybody else did. Nobody could understand this. And it really was a big thing, since my family ate ice cream quite often. And it's also interesting, I just thought that I sort of felt I had to like a flavor, so I'd choose one flavor for awhile until I got sick of it and then I'd choose another. But I did begin to like ice cream more, and I think it's right around when I went away to college and afterwards, when I was out of home, and also when I began to eat some flavors that were sort of novel and unheard of in my home, since we always had the same old good basic choices. [silence] It's funny, too, that for years and years I've been aware that this same thing that works in my family, of sort of that togetherness because you're choosing the same things and enjoying the same ideas, doesn't work outside of the family. And even though I knew it didn't, I couldn't do anything about it; even though I knew it would drive my friends crazy that all I'd do is agree and follow sort of their choices and tastes. And I didn't even want to be that way—frustrated me as much as it frustrated anybody else. But still, even though I knew this, that was the way I functioned both inside and outside of the family. And I think that's one of the things that makes it so hard for me to be with my parents now and particularly my father. He's— my mother will just sort of enjoy a good fight if we disagree politically, and [clears throat] she's not so emotional if you do agree and so forth. But my father really, practically—tears will come to his eyes. It's not quite that bad, but that's the way I think he's feeling inside, if you agree, and if for no other reason. Right now I'm feeling I can't agree just because it sickens me to have to go through.this whole thing. And yet I know it hurts him and it's sort of needless to hurt somebody.

She is searching in the past for explanations of her behavior. She speaks of domination by her parents and her father's need to have her share his feelings. She is "sickened" by that, the same word she used in describing the sexual episode with her husband (p. 32).

We can speculate on the possibility that the patient regards the analyst as being like her father, who demands conformity to his views and tastes as a condition for closeness. This might explain the patient's paralysis at the beginning of the session. It could be a kind of protest against a demand that she conform to the analyst's expectation that she should be the one to speak and that she should verbalize whatever is on her mind. She did, after all, perceive him as impatient at the door (presumably because of some slight deviance on her part from the manner or the speed with which she thought he expected her to enter). These speculations, however, are far less grounded than they might be had the analyst pursued the explicit and implicit relationship themes that we have commented on prior to this point. An exploration of the patient's experience of the relationship with the analyst in the here-and-now might have set the stage, eventually, for interpretations connecting the analyst to the father. Of course, the associations about the father might not have come up at this point, or even in this session, had the analyst pursued the here-and-now expressions of the transference. It seems likely, however, that they would come up eventually, and they would then stand a better chance of being meaningfully interpreted in the context of the transference.

A: [cough]

P: Because I think I was just thinking that F had wanted this weekend to go to Z [place]. And, and I just really haven't wanted to go, as much as I like Z, and I thought of all kinds of excuses — that it really won't be very nice up there and that the drive up and back is horrible and I can't face it, especially after the accident we had and the awful time we had driving it. And, but really basically I think it's just I don't want to see my parents and if they're up there I just don't want to be there. And his family wants us to come to their home, and usually both of us much prefer to go to my parents than to his, and here we have the perfect opportunity. And I think I'd prefer to go to his family, because somehow I'm not involved emotionally. And just that fact, even though I may not like a lot of things that are happening, makes me feel much more relaxed and happy. So now I'm happy with his family and he's happy with mine.

Again we hear about wanting to remain emotionally uninvolved, as was true in the sexual episode. One can only speculate on how the matter of involvement may relate to the analytic situation. So far the analyst's overt involvement, in speech at any rate, has been confined to an early question (p. 32).

P: There's something else too. I think that I was just thinking of an evening when they were at our apartment for dinner — his family [cough]. And, um, I've always thought his mother says some very stupid things and is a very difficult person to get along with anyway, because she just sort of monopolizes things and doesn't even listen to somebody else. And I've just always kind of let her rattle on because there's not much else you can do. But F used to be very fond of her and sort of blind to this, and it used to really bother me that he didn't see this side of her, because it was so blatant to me. And now he's beginning to see it and it drives him crazy, the way she'll carry on. And I think I get some kind of sadistic pleasure out of that. And that's one reason why I, aside from the other things I've said, I like going. Because then it sort of is making it clear to F how, I suppose, I'm better than his mother.

One could suspect an allusion to the analyst via identification. She may feel he lets her rattle on because there's not much else he can do.

P: [two-minute silence] It's funny how today everything seems to be running in terms of, of, of my ha —, ha —, sort of my looking at how I have in the past, and probably still do, seek approval and disapproval or feel it. And yet today I felt very much that I, I could sort of, well, like when I'm shopping, admit when I didn't know exactly what I wanted or I didn't know [cough] exactly how to use something and, well, just simply admit my ignorance. And I used to always feel that I couldn't admit it, especially in things like if I'm buying makeup or something, because then the saleswoman will be very scornful: "Why don't you know these things? How can you be ignorant?" And so then I wouldn't buy them just because I'd be afraid of admitting ignorance. And today I; it didn't bother me and no —, and it didn't strike me anybody was scornful either.

She reflects on what she has been saying and tries to integrate it. She may be taking over the role of analyst because he has failed to take any initiative. She was silent for two minutes before these last remarks, perhaps hoping for some response from him.

A: It's interesting in light of the dream that you had Saturday night and in light of the way you describe your feelings of your sexual experience with F. Because in the dream you were very worried and in the end felt your ignorance — not knowing how to handle the puppet or not being able to handle the puppet — uh, persisted. But that dream followed the experience in which what you emphasized, what you emphasized about it was that you wanted to, that you couldn't enjoy yourself and you wanted to satisfy F. I think there must some connection between wanting to masturbate him and this dream about the puppet. And the feeling that you couldn't do with the puppet what needed to be done. You couldn't perform with it.

It's hard to know what the analyst is driving at. What is clear is that he proposes a connection between the sexual episode and the dream about the puppet, that he wishes to emphasize her inability to perform, and that he is hinting at something about masturbation.

P: And my mind jumps to: if there is a connection it would be the fear that if we, if I involve myself wanting intercourse and then couldn't have an orgasm, or the fear that I wouldn't be able to, or that that would be the parallel that — I suppose that sort of reflects on the whole way I've been feeling today. And that I didn't, whatever it was, I didn't want to risk it. I didn't want to just say, "Oh, well, we can try and if we, if I can't, so what? If I can, so what?" Because very often when I have felt in that mood, when it's been not, not colored by sort of feeling guilt at having a definite attraction toward F, then I've been very bothered if I haven't been able to have an orgasm. I've been very frustrated and I don't have the attitude: "Well, so what?" Sort of, like that's the one and only chance and I failed. But I wasn't at all aware of feeling that way. Yet I suppose that must be part of it because if I felt guilt at just wanting to have the sexual experience, then I should — or just sort of liking nudeness, which I used to find very hard to admit — then I probably wouldn't have even wanted to masturbate F.

What she says is not very clear. She does focus on the analyst's suggestion that she could not perform and relates it to a fear that she might not have an orgasm, but it all seems speculative. The transference, moreover, is not touched upon by either the patient or the analyst.

A: What was the puppet like?

An unexpected change of direction. The analyst had apparently begun to develop an interpretation of the dream and now he returns to the manifest content for further detail, probably to pave the way for something he intends to say.

P: It's funny. I, I, I can recall enough to know that while I was practicing with it, playing with it, it had a very definite character and face and so forth. And now all I can remember is that it was, the hand puppet type that you put your hand up inside and it, it's like a glove or a mitten over your hand. But I know that it had much more than that and I'm left with the feeling that I had at the end of the dream, which was, "What is this thing? What can I bring out about it? It's faceless." And that's what it, that's what I recall now.
A: Do you think you could have thought of it as a penis?

It seems clear that what the analyst says is not derived so much from the patient's associations to his question as from what he had in mind in the change of direction above. The "facelessness" may have been confirming, though, of his hypothesis.

P: Well, when you said what kind of a puppet it was, then I thought of a hand puppet and then of masturbating F. I did make that connection. But it was—I, I don't—it's the first time I'd thought of it in that way.
A: You didn't say that thought, right?
P: You mean you think I've thought it before?
A: No, I mean you—you said that you had just thought of it when I first brought it up?
P: Well, more in terms of I thought that's what you're driving at. [chuckle]

A: Ha, yeah, right. But, but you didn't mention it.

The patient chuckles, and it is not hard to understand why. The exchange is an enactment of the struggle over who takes initiative. The analyst wants her to admit responsibility for connecting the puppet to penis and masturbation, but she turns the responsibility back on him by saying she is merely divining what he was driving at.

The exchange also suggests an enactment of a conflict about conforming to the analyst's expectations, similar, perhaps, to the conflict in the patient's relationship with her father. In this instance, she withholds a thought that she no doubt imagines the therapist would be pleased to hear. The analyst, in turn, assumes what could readily be construed by the patient as a critical, impatient, manipulative stance (reminiscent of the patient's perception of him at the door, of her relationship with her father, and of the puppet dream).

P: No. I immediately go to this defensive reaction that it's too far-fetched. I mean, when I think about it, it all fits together. [pause] And I think somehow somewhere in the back of my mind— I can't recall now exactly what feelings I had about my reaction to my class on Thursday and the dream I had about my instructor, but I, I right now am thinking in terms that I feel still confused by what all that meant. And so when I had this dream, and it was in terms of a class and puppets and so forth, I sort of went, "Aha, another clue to what was happening in this other situation," and so that's always the light I was looking at it in.

A: Yeah. Well, but the sequence of your thoughts essentially was: You go to the movie, and the way you described it was that you saw the man's genitals. You saw him naked. Right?

P: Uh-hum.

A: And then your focus is that during your sexual experience with F you wanted to masturbate him. And then later that night you dream you have a puppet that you can't make perform.

The patient begins to develop what her line of thinking had

been in relation to the dream, but the analyst seems bent on imposing his own view, despite the fact that she labels the particular detail he is pushing "far-fetched." Now they actually seem to be competing over who will determine the direction they will take. She may well experience the therapist as insisting she conform to his wishes and abandon her effort to make her own choices.

P: And it wasn't just once during the weekend that I felt that way. I felt that way Sunday too. No, I can see that. But it, um, I think I was going to— going back now to just what was happening when I had this reaction, when I had the dream, and the other dream, and then the reaction I did in class. [pause] I think maybe part of this feeling is simply, well, I don't know, I can't quite get my finger on it. But it has something to do with if I, if the dream was just purely and simply fantasizing about my instructor or about you [cough] and having a sexual experience, I can't, I just can't tolerate thinking that I was even fantasizing something like that, unless what it really means is that it's symbolic of somebody else. I think I said this on Friday too, that if it represented my father or F then I could accept it, but this is why I have to keep going back to it and it has been disturbing me. It's almost as if I can't let it alone until I make it mean something that I can then accept that it means, until I can sort of pattern it, work it around, fit it into some form that I can stand. [silence]

Now she is saying something that she truly owns as her own and is presenting her experience of the relationship. She can't stand the idea that she might have sexual ideas relating to the analyst as himself.

P: Again, it's just I get to this point and then I can't go any further. I think that happened to me practically at this point on Friday too, and I started to think of, um, well sort of, more or less of school. And I was thinking of something that occurred to me sometime recently, about part of the trouble I was having after Christmas, I think, was sort of a strong reaction to things that I think bothered me when I was growing and I didn't want to do the same with the children. So I overreacted. For instance, in giving any kind of criticism, I wanted to make them feel whatever they wanted to do was all right, and lots of freedom of choice. And I just took away all the structure because I didn't feel any structure. I didn't know what I thought was right and what I didn't, and I was so afraid of hurting them the way I think I've been hurt, or at least the way I reacted and was hurt, whether or not it was really being done to me. And in a way I was hurting the children by sort of not giving them any direction at all. But I don't really want to think about this. Because when I'm talking about— I just sort of find I'm not really interested in it and . . .

The opening theme of the hour—a conflict about taking initiative and giving direction—has returned in manifest form. There are doubtless important connections between this theme and the sexual one. She probably feels that to take initiative is equivalent to owning to sexual desire, as when she became aroused in relation to her husband. It is this equivalence which might explain her conflict about initiative in the analytic situation. The conflict is experienced here in terms of her feeling about the children. Because of her wish not to dominate them as she feels she was dominated, she overreacts and deprives them of any structure. She may well experience the analyst as behaving similarly in relation to her. It may well be that the experience of the relationship must be clarified first in these terms before the specifically sexual theme can be usefully addressed. Her statement that she can go no further (p. 43, line 31) is a request for help from the analyst.

At some level she may feel that the analyst is frozen himself and cannot help precisely because he is struggling with a sexual wish toward her. She may have the idea that the reason he does not encourage her to elaborate on her sexual interest in him, or indeed on any issue in the transference, is that such "initiative" has sexual meaning for him too.

A: Well, as you said, your thoughts go back to the dream

about the instructor and you're thinking about him and about me and that's where you're sort of stuck, unresolved.

P: Because it just struck me: Why does it bother me so much if it remains unresolved? Why can't it just be unresolved?

A: There was a feature of that dream that you didn't say anything about and this was that you weren't sure whether you were alone. Does that bring anything to mind?

The analyst's remark in the first lines above seems like a beginning responsiveness to the patient's experience, but his subsequent question about the dream is jarring. It may be a beginning replay of the interaction he started earlier (p. 41), leading to the question of whether the puppet could represent a penis. He is again taking the initiative away from her and perhaps asking her to divine what he has in mind. There is even some question about the accuracy of his recollection of the dream. It was not that she was not sure whether she was alone but that she didn't remember whether anyone was "running the class"—again, a reference to who has the initiative, who is in charge.

P: It brings to mind something that has occurred to me this weekend that was in, um, *Portnoy's Complaint*, when one of the mistresses that he had was talking about, well—it was also an experience they had of having more than two people there. And then when she was talking about a couple who asked her to watch them while they had intercourse, and sort of this element of an audience. And that thought kept occurring to me almost as if I wanted it, and in a sort of perverse way. And yet I wouldn't want it at all. But. And it also made me think of, um, how back in the fall whenever F and I had intercourse, I would always— well, I don't know exactly how I thought of it then, but somewhere in the thoughts either right then or afterwards would be: "Now I'll have to talk about it here." So it was almost as if you could be there watching us. But, yet this liking of nudeness and, and being able to be nude myself now without feeling the way I used to, or generally without feeling the way I used to—it's almost as if now I don't care if there's another person or not. I'm not hiding in the way I was.

A: Well, our time's up.

The analyst seems to have hit on something, but it's not clear what it is. The idea that the analyst is watching her and her husband in intercourse may be as close as she can come to a conscious fantasy of intercourse with the analyst. Undoubtedly, additional meanings are possible, but the data permit no more than speculation. One should, however, consider another possible allusion — to the recording. Patient and analyst are performing in public.

ADDITIONAL COMMENTS

The hour starts with a four-minute silence, followed by an account of the difficulty the patient experiences in beginning to speak. She then describes a vivid experience which occurred when the analyst opened the door. She perceived him as impatient and critical, although she says nothing about what she imagines he was impatient or critical about. In retrospect, we know that a four-minute silence followed this encounter at the door. The analyst allows this rather charged opening to pass without comment. There follows an account of a situation in which the patient is conflicted about asserting herself and taking initiative, a report of a sexual experience in which she suddenly became inhibited after feeling aroused, and a description of a dream with probable allusions to the theme of conflict about initiative in both the sexual and the analytic situations. The analyst makes no response and the patient turns to other topics in which the same theme seems clearly implied. When the hour is about two-thirds over the analyst turns to the dream with a somewhat obscure remark suggesting the sexual implications of its manifest content. The patient catches the implication and there ensues a brief struggle in which each imputes responsibility for the idea to the other. The patient then begins to integrate the data on her own and expresses her distress at the idea that she might explicitly fantasize a sexual relationship with the analyst. One wonders what has made this possible. Perhaps just the degree of initiative the analyst has taken has been enough to enable the patient to reveal more. It seems unlikely that it is the quality of his interventions that is responsible for the forward movement. The hour ends with the analyst apparently returning to an enactment of the struggle over initiative rather than an exploration of it.

A much earlier discussion of the dream—without preconceived ideas of its meaning, but with an eye to possible allusions to the transference, bridging the issues of her difficulties in getting started in the hour and in the sexual episode—would probably have been much more effective in promoting the analytic process. We also emphasize that the initial, apparently superficial, and relatively brief explicit reference to her experience of the relationship—that is, the difficulty in getting started—could have been the analyst's first cue as to the nature of the transference issues warranting exploration. In addition, had the analyst focused on it, the patient's fleeting impression of him as standing impatiently at the door as she entered (which is never mentioned again by either party) might well have opened the way to an exploration of the principal issues in the patient's experience of the interaction in this hour.

3

PATIENT C: SESSION 95

INTRODUCTION

In this session the analyst starts to intervene when the session is about half over. His intervention begins with an extra-transference intrapsychic interpretation, to which the patient responds angrily. The analyst then interprets the transference in the same idiom that characterized the original extra-transference interpretation, instead of taking the immediate interaction into account and recognizing how that interaction accounts for the patient's experience of the relationship from her point of view. The analyst would have had a clue to how the patient experienced his contribution to the transference if he had been aware of the probable allusions to the transference in the extra-transference material of the first half of the session.

This session also illustrates the distinction between interpreting a reference to behavior outside as an acting out of the transference and interpreting it as an allusion to the same interaction within the transference. The irony of the situation is that there is enough truth in the extra-transference interpretation to force the patient to acknowledge it. This seeming agreement supports the analyst's belief that he is on the right track and simultaneously blinds him to the way his own behavior contributes to a transference-countertransference enactment of an aspect of the patient's neurosis and the typical response she elicits from others.

THE ANNOTATED SESSION

P: I remember that you mentioned it and then I didn't get it.

What this refers to does not become clear.

P: We're rehearsing today. And I love to rehearse. And, uh, it

49

doesn't seem unreasonable to me to leave two and a half hours. But I'm getting a lot of static [inaudible] from J [boss]. He seems to use two things when he wants, when he wants to get at me. We had a huge fight last night. Such a, such a big fight, that I ended up crying in front of, at him, crying and screaming at him. And G [boyfriend] was there, and H [woman], and J's wife, L. But the crying finally got him. I didn't really do it on purpose. I just was very overwrought. But every time I'd get in an argument with him, he smirks and he says, "Are you having your period?" That and my coming up here are the two things that he waves at me. Like when I left today, I mean, I told him all day, that I was, you know. Yesterday, he calls up in the middle of the afternoon yesterday, and he decided that G's volunteering to help was an arch-insult and that it's just full of shit. And that he didn't want to have anything to do with it and so he was going to come over and work with me. And then we were going to rehearse today. And I said, "OK. That's fine." I said, "Well, you know, I'll be leaving for a couple of hours in the afternoon." He said, "Why, where do you have to go?" And I said, "I have to go to the shrink." And then he said, "Oh my God." He's always going on like that. And it was interesting, when he called to tell me that, that he decided that uh, G's offer was, uh, an insult and a putdown. The first thing he said [inaudible]— he called while I was gone, while I was here yesterday, and when I got back I got the message. And I call him up and he says, "Hello," and I say, "Hello," and he said, "Well, how is the shrink? [voice raised] I just can't understand what it is, tell me what it is that compels you to go up there four times a week. Tell me what's so interesting about it. I only wish I'd made a pact with the devil, so that I would do something like that four times a week, like going to the movies. Think how many movies I would see. Now tell me what it is it does for you." He had a long speech like that. And, uh, then launched right into the thing about how he decided that it was all bullshit. So, M was there today too. I don't know that she knew where I was going. And she probably thought it was a little odd that I left [inaudible].

You know, I was thinking about it, feeling shitty about it on the train, because J was probably giving her a big number about how much time I spend coming and going. And he said yesterday, "You don't even, you don't have time to do anything. How can you spend all that time?" [sigh] [inaudible] He's just so gross about it. Like he's always yelling and screaming and embarrassing me.

She details how someone else attacks the analysis. Perhaps she is putting her complaints in his mouth, but at present this can only be a speculation, which the analyst should keep to himself unless he has evidence to support it from earlier sessions.

P: The thing last night started out with, uh, you know, working on something, and he'd say, "Well, then we'll be able to do this and that." I said, "Which one are we going to do?" [inaudible] say, "Well, we can do it this way or that way." I said, "Yeah, but I've got to know which one we're going to do." He said, "I don't know already. What's the matter with you?" I said, "Nothing is the matter with me. I just don't want, I just want to get this down, you know. I haven't got, I want to get the story really firm so I can go and do the sketches." And he was saying, like, you know, the figures are too big, the this, and he doesn't want to do it this way, and, and, uh, the background should be some other way, and, like, wanting to change everything. Things that I've done all along and that he's seen. And what it finally seemed to boil down to was, you know, I want to know almost as much about how it's going to be directed as he knows. I have to know that to make the sketches right. And I'm very fearful about these long scenes. Because they're not just, you know, one static tableau or anything. They really, you know, they have a lot of movement in them, and things. And so I keep asking him things, and he'd say, "You give me a front view of this—the teacher here." There's a scene with a teacher and a little kid. And I said, well, you know, "What's the scene going to be? What's it going to look like and then what's going to happen next?" I said, "Why don't you go through the whole thing and tell

me like how you see it happening." And so finally I just —
what really got me — was I kept asking him to tell me what
the thing was about. And all he would do was say, "You'll
give me this, you'll give me that."

It seems possible that there are allusions to the analysis here
having to do with some feeling that she's being asked for a lot
but working in the dark or some sense of being subservient to
unnecessary secrecy about the analyst's aims. But again there
are no preceding references to the analysis to provide a basis for
such suggestions. One can only wait and watch for further clues.

P: And he was really mad at me too. And I was really mad at
him. He's just such a fucking egomaniac, I can't stand it.
You know, I finally worked out, sort of, well, you know, I
mean after the big outburst you know, he was, what he
said was, "Oh, it's so, so beautiful. Your crying is so
beautiful." [inaudible] "What's so beautiful about it?" And
he said, "It's so human." And I said, "You, you've doubted
all this time that I'm human?" I said, "Oh it's just, it's so
fantastic." You know, he's just that kind of a guy. And uh,
you know — so he seemed to be sort of stunned by that. I
mean, I didn't even know how much turmoil there was. It
was just that I had like, oh, three, or four, or five days to
stew about it and worry. And the whole thing got, you
know, built up to that intensity.

A: What about your crying?

P: What about it?

A: What made you, what made you cry?

P: Uh, I get so furious at his not believing what I was telling
him. That I needed to know. And at his continually telling
me to, you know, keep quiet. You know, it was, like, just
out of frustration. Yeah, I mean, this guy, when he wants
to make a point, you can't, you literally cannot get a sentence in. He will outyell you. And if you start to say something, you can never finish a sentence. Because by the time
you got the sentence half out, he thinks he knows what the
rest of the sentence is, and oftentimes he does know. But he
just, you know, he keeps saying [voice raised], "Now listen

to me, look at me, listen to me." Like that. Then he kept
saying [voice raised], "I want you to shut up and listen to
me and listen to what I'm telling you." And I kept saying,
"But you don't understand, you don't understand what I
want. You don't understand what I, you know, what I
need to know about this." And he said, "Just shut up, just
shut up." You know, I, he was really, you know, unbeliev-
able.

One might think that the analyst's relative silence makes him an
unlikely candidate as a figure implicitly alluded to here, but the
patient could still be experiencing him in this way. We are ad-
mittedly anticipating what is to come.

P: And the first thing that pissed me off was his, his insisting
     that I change my attitude. And he said, "What's, you
     know, what's the matter with you?" And he said, "You're,
     you know, you're not acting the way you've always acted."
     And I said, well, you know, "I'm not. I want to get this
     done, and I'm not in a particularly jolly mood. And some-
     times people's moods just don't fit in with the way you want
     them to be." And I said, "You just have to accept that."
     And he said, "That's a lot of shit." And I said, well, "Come
     on, let's, you know, let's keep doing this." And the other
     thing that [chuckle] he sort of looked a little embarrassed
     about and laughed at was that he was saying he didn't like
     my attitude. And I said, "Yes, I'm not acting like I love you
     every minute." And he said, "No, no it's just that we've
     been working so well before and I don't understand, you
     know, I don't understand why you're behaving this way.
     And, you know, why you act the way you did before. You
     know, we're going to keep a pleasant working relationship."
     I said, "Yeah, the only way that it's pleasant is for me to act
     the way I, as if I love you all the time." So anyway, so to-
     day everything was fine, you know. Until I said I was go-
     ing to leave, like, and I warned him ahead of time. And I
     said, you know, "Let's do this." And H was working with
     him. It's not like I left him by himself. And H knows how
     everything is supposed to be done and where everything is

and all that. And, uh, the thing, another thing that pissed me off was he made it like, he made it look like I was leaving for all afternoon, you know, while P [woman] was there, and I said. . .

A: This was going on at your house?

P: Last night.

A: Not today?

P: No, no, the rehearsal is. . .

A: The rehearsal is where?

P: On X Street. I left there too early. Because the last time I came up here from the library, I was late. It took me, like, an hour and ten minutes. So I left at 12:30. I got up here at ten after one. Anyway. So we were going along just fine and, uh, I was, at 12 o'clock I said, well, "Listen, I'm going to be leaving in about half an hour." And he, you know, he said, "OK." And so at 12:30 I said—you know, I put on my coat—and I said, well, "All right, listen, I'll see you a little later." And he said, he went, uh, he made a face, he went "tsk" [sighs and makes disgusted noise]. Oh, like that, sort of, you know, and smirked, and he said, "Well, have a nice day." I said, "Listen, I'll be back by three o'clock. So, you know, don't worry about it." But it just. . . [a few inaudible words]. My fantasy is that when I get back he is going to, you know—P will be there, everybody'll be there—and J will say, "Well, how was the shrink?" You know. He just has no fucking discretion whatsoever about anything. If he comes into the house, yelling at the top of his lungs—I don't really like yelling in the house. I don't like yelling in general. Although I do it. I don't like other people yelling. [inaudible] Like the other night he came in and he was yelling and talking very loudly and singing and hollering and I said, I said, "Hey, you know, I'm right here, cut the volume a little." And he said, "Why? Who's asleep?" I said, "Nobody's asleep, I just, you know, don't like yelling in the house." He said, "What? Don't tell me to shush." You know, he really doesn't give a shit what anybody else wants or thinks. And every time I disagree with him, he thinks it's G's doing. That G has goaded me into it.

The possibility is worth considering that she feels the analyst experiences her the way she experiences J, that is, that the analyst finds her loud and indiscreet. In other words, she may be alluding to the analyst via identification.

P: Oh, like this morning I— when we're doing the scene with the teacher and the little kid, we've been using a blackboard. But because we don't have our sets yet, somebody has to hold it up all the time. So we had been talking about temporarily getting a device where we can, like, put it up and lean it, like, on or against something, so that we didn't have to have a person standing there holding the thing all the time. So [inaudible] we were down there getting ready to do the scene, and I said, ah, "Are we going to have to go through this holding the blackboard trip again?" And he said, "Oh God!" I said, "What's the matter? I just asked." And he said, "I hear G talking there. That's G talking, that's not you." I said, "Gee, J, if you just forget about G for a few minutes you'd probably be a lot more comfortable." You know, it's a combination of, I have a feeling on one hand he thinks I'm mindless and on the other hand, you know— and, and mindless and, and, uh, driven by G's every whim. And on the other he, he thinks that I'm much too strong-minded. I'm giving him a lot of trouble, you know; it's got to such a point now where even, even when we say we like each other, I don't feel that we do. You know, I'm, I'm just so, so very sensitive to being picked on in little ways I just, it just doesn't roll off my back very well. [inaudible] He's the sort of person where if he knows you're sensitive about something, he'll rub it in your face, rub your nose in it—salt in the wound—instead of trying to be nice about it. You know, I mean, he, he just thinks he can decide how everybody is to behave.

These perceptions of J could be displaced from the analyst. Her feeling that J considers her to be at once mindless and too strong-minded and feels that she gives him a lot of trouble could be an allusion to how she believes the analyst feels about her. The remarks about how J rubs salt into a wound may also allude to what she feels the analyst does.

A: So what about salt?

P: What?

A: I said, "What about salt on the wound?"

P: Ah yes, the great aching wounds. Also rubbing your nose in it, which is what I don't, I remember talking about, um. . .

A: Because you take his comments about you having to go to the shrink four times a week, as, as if he were saying, "Boy, there must be plenty wrong with you, that you have to do that."

The analyst's question about salt on the wound is unclear here. It doubtless refers to something they mutually understood from earlier sessions. Material later in this session suggests an allusion to the female genital conceived of as a wound. The patient's reply already hints at the sarcasm and despair with which she will deal with this idea.

P: Yes, sort of, except I— I know that. I think one thing that he resents about it is that he knows I'm—this may sound weird—but he knows I'm talking to somebody else instead of talking to him. And the reason I think that is because he likes to know what everybody's up to and he likes to, you know, know where they're at. And I think he considers it like a threat to him. Just the way he considers, you know, my talking to G about things a threat. Anytime anybody makes, you know, yells at the top of their lungs about my seeing a shrink, I don't like it. I was very embarrassed when T [male] said it. I mean it's not something I'm particularly proud of, you know. [pause] You know, with people, with people I know, it's cool but— or with people that I feel comfortable with I guess is a better thing. And I guess what it is, is people that I think are going to stick with me till I get fixed, you see. I remember the thing I didn't like about T saying it was that it's like I assumed that everybody else would say, "Oh, we wouldn't, we're not going to have to pay attention to her, you know. Poor crazy girl."

A: She doesn't have anything worth paying attention to.

P: All right, if you want to put it that way. Or did I already put it that way? You know, I'm getting sick of this. Every-time we come back to the same thing and then [inaudible] just stops there. Mental block. Done this routine many times before. I'm thinking of knocking all the books off the wall again. So what about it?

The analyst now more clearly refers to the female genital. The patient's response provides us with data which make plausible the inference that the earlier material about the dictatorial man alludes to the analyst implicitly. Even her saying, "All right, if you want to put it that way," suggests that she feels he insists on directing every detail. She is sick of what she experiences as his reiterating this point which still leaves her "in the dark" — i.e., does not contribute to her progress in dealing with the issue. She responds with an angry wish to knock his books off the wall, perhaps because she feels he is mechanically following some for-mula taken right from a book.

A: What about knocking all the books off there?
P: It's, I'm getting mad. I'm lying here getting mad and I'm afraid to move because I'm mad. I mean, what it seems like — and I know it's worked — but what it seems like is that you're always, no matter what I say, you're always bring-ing it back to this, you know — my thing about something being wrong with me. And then we just get to that, and then nothing fucking happens. We just end up saying, "Well, you think there's something wrong with you." So big fucking deal. What about it? You know, when are we go-ing to get away from the illness and onto the cure? [sigh] Huh? [phone rings] [several inaudible words]

The plausibility of the inference that she experiences him as dic-tatorial is even greater now. He too, like J, keeps harping on one theme. Perhaps even the earlier reference to J's smirking re-mark about her periods is applicable.

A: [inaudible] — I take the idea about knocking all the books off the wall as if you wanted to knock my penis off.

An almost unbelievably pat interpretation that exemplifies our point. Instead of finding out what she means by wanting to knock down his books, the analyst uses what she has said to reiterate his fixed conviction, which—however correct it may be—she has just characterized as unhelpful. It is far more likely that her conscious experience is that he is repeating a formula from his books and that that is why she wants to knock them down.

P: You do?
A: Yes, I do.
P: [laugh]
A: That your reaction to my saying it is to want to do that.
P: Is to want to be [inaudible]—what?
A: Is to want to do that.
P: Well, if that's what getting mad is.
A: It wasn't just getting mad. It was also knocking all the books off the wall.
P: But why, but why are books a penis now? [sigh] Huh? Yeah, I think I always thought they were. That's why I read so much. I'm serious and I'm saying it sarcastically, but think back about trying to be smart.
A: Yeah, I know.
P: [inaudible]—OK. Well, I'm admitting it ruefully, but I'm admitting it pissed-offedly. [inaudible] If I can't have one, you can't have one either? And if you won't give me one, then you can't have yours. But it's still the same question. And it's still the same feeling. Take that lamp, for example.

What contributes to her dilemma is that she realizes the interpretation has its own plausibility. She has always tried to be smart and she recognizes that her wish to knock down his books may be because of envy of his knowledge. But the interpretation fails to help her just as she complained it failed to help her before (p. 56). Ironically, the fact that she does see some plausibility in the interpretation—and indeed it doubtless does have some—may well confirm the analyst's belief that his work is correct and good. He will see the problem as her resistance rather than as his failure to address what is meaningful to her in the here-and-now, i.e., her experience of him as an unreasonable dictator and the basis for her experience in his actual behavior.

A: But at the moment J is a convenient target, I would think.

P: Yes, he's a convenient target because he really is a prick.

A: Yeah. He lords it over you.

P: That's right.

A: And he's very easy to get mad at.

P: That's true. Yeah, I feel like, you know, what you're saying is that I'm mad at J when I'm really mad at you. And that you want me to be mad at you, really, and admit that I'm really mad at you, and that if I won't admit it, then I'm, you know, denying you that, which is mean.

She experiences his interpretation as suggesting an acting out of the transference—getting angry with J instead of the analyst because J is a convenient target. An alternative view, we suggest, is that her anger at J may well be appropriate in its own right and that, as was explained in Volume I, she *associated* about J because it provided her a way of implicitly alluding to her anger at the analyst for his lording it over her (her experience of his reiterated unhelpful interpretation). She is, of course, not conscious that this played a role in determining her associations. What the analyst should interpret is that her talk about J is also an allusion to how she experiences him. Ideally, he should not only point to the parallel between her experience of his interpretation and her reactions to J, but also clarify that her experience of the analytic siutation can be understood in light of how she interprets the analyst's behavior.

P: [sigh] Do you really think this is all about penises? Or do you just think it because you're a man and, and a Freudian? You know, I mean, I wonder sometimes. You never said you were a Freudian; I assume that you are. Always showing me those dirty pictures [several inaudible words]. Maybe this is all because of that couple of days when I decided you were so brilliant and I knew I would have to get into combat again. So I knew I would have to get into combat again. So I was just going to say, "I don't think you like me," and that what I, what I was thinking before was that, after all this time, I still don't like you. I thought I didn't like you first.

Her remark about the analyst's being a Freudian confirms our earlier suggestion that the presenting meaning of her wanting to knock his books down is that his interpretation is a rote one from a book. Again, the irony of the situation is that she recognizes a possible motive for attacking him as stemming from her envy of his "brilliance," which lends credence to his interpretation. This may bespeak a masochistic surrender, which will remain undealt with so long as she experiences his interpretation as a sadistic assault and he remains oblivious to the plausibility of her experiencing it that way. (Her reference to "dirty pictures" may be an allusion to an old joke about the Rorschach: the patient sees genitals everywhere and when the tester asks her how come, she asks why he shows her these dirty pictures. If this is the allusion, it is another example of the patient taking the responsibility for her response entirely upon herself. The point of the story is that the responsibility for seeing sex everywhere is projected onto the tester.)

A: No, I think you're afraid that, you know, when we started to talk about this that you— what comes up is how angry you feel at [inaudible]. . .

P: Yes, at you?

A: Men. And you are frightened that you won't be liked.

She was willing to stay with their relationship, but he generalizes to men. Furthermore, he shifts to a new theme—her fear that she won't be liked—and throws the responsibility on her for what is going on. In the meantime, he ignores her very direct statement of her dislike for him and her conviction—not fear—that he does not like her.

P: I never was. "When you get to college, dear, boys will like you," my mother said. I don't think she said "boys will like you"—that's what I, that's what I felt it really meant. But she said that you'll find boys that you like, that you have more in common with. You see, [inaudible] be based on common interest and good healthy things like that couldn't be based on [raises voice] fucking and sex—[inaudible] to be something nice. It had to be a real relationship, not just sex. Shit.

These remarks are somewhat difficult to understand. Perhaps if the words omitted because they could not be made out from the tape were there it would be clearer. She is sarcastic about her mother's espousal of a "real relationship" rather than "just sex." At the same time, perhaps she is siding with her mother against the analyst's single-mindedly pushing a purely sexual interpretation. She may wish the analyst would like her and be interested in her as a whole person, rather than always pursuing his ideas about her penis envy. The result is a relationship that does not seem real to her.

P: You know, I feel like I'm going to be released from this room and that I'm going to be raging, in a raging fury, and nobody will know why. [laugh] [inaudible] I just walk along, you know, nice and straight. If I get angry enough all at once, then would I get over it? Primal scream. I can't imagine, you know, feeling really, feeling like there isn't anything wrong with me. I was thinking about that the other day. What would it be like, you know, to feel that you really just, you know, you were where you ought to be, and everything is just really full?

She may be implying that the analyst doesn't really know why she is angry.

P: [pause] Just thought of my brother again. I don't think anything in particular. I just thought of [inaudible].
A: Well, what about him?
P: His existence. I was thinking about men. I was wondering whether or not, you know, whether it really— first I was thinking, well, "Is this sort of a chauvinistic position to decide that, you know, women really want to be like men, and they're pissed-off that they don't have cocks?" And what I was thinking about [yawn]— whether that was

really true or whether you know what the story really is. And I was thinking about— because, you know, I don't feel that I've ever been particularly dumped on. And I was thinking of men that I knew. [inaudible] Thought of my brother, because we talked about him before. It's weird, because I never really thought of my brother very much until, you know—I mean, when we were kids I did. But I never really thought of him as a figure in my life, an influence. I always thought that I was the stronger personality. But I think the reason I thought that is because I had to think that. [pause]

Again, the doubt as to whether penis envy is the real story. Nevertheless, she is willing to consider that her conscious life-long feeling about her brother is a denial. She enacts a submission to the analyst.

A: You mean: as if to deny that, you envy him anything.

The analyst is only too ready to accept this confirmation of his view. He ignores the doubt, probably considering it a persisting resistance.

P: Right. And that I started doing that so early that I never even really thought of it, you know, never entered my mind, probably never left my mind. Ha. The meaning of the madness. So, you know, I mean, what I'm thinking is that I don't even have the balls to be mad. You know, I wonder what that means. And it is, you know, in the realm of events, like it is conceivable that I can rise up off this couch and rip a couple of shelves off the wall. But I just would never do it, I don't think. I want. But I just really couldn't do it. Why couldn't I really do it? It's either I'd feel like an ass, or either I would feel—ah, yes, great deal of anger had built up in me and it would certainly justify to rip down the shelves on the wall. And I'd have to think that you thought that. You know—what a good healthy act. And that just seemed like bullshit to think that.

She is enraged. At the same time she acknowledges her subservience by saying she could not display her anger in a physical way unless she thought he would approve.

P: Snap up the couch like a folding bed—me in it.
A: I'm not clear about that image about the couch. I would snap up...
P: No, I would. I would make it snap up so I could disappear.
A: Snap up how?
P: Like those folding beds [makes noise], like that. Snap it into a jelly roll. Jelly rolls, black blues music, a synonym for pussy.
A: Yes, I know.
P: You know a lot. Well, I just want to tell you in case you didn't know. [pause] [sigh] What's folding bed mean? Back to the womb?

Perhaps she feels so vanquished that she wants to disappear. She makes what sounds like a mocking association to pussy. The interaction between them then becomes a replay of what has been going on. She explains something to him, but he reasserts his dominance, saying he already knows. She sarcastically alludes to his know-it-all attitude and then out-Freuds him by coming up with another cliché interpretation (about the womb).

A: And also it sounds like some image of using the vagina in such a way as to snap something out.
P: Back to the womb?
A: [several inaudible words]—since it's jelly roll that comes to your mind.
P: [laugh] Well, at least then I think that I have one. Yeah, but what does that mean using that as my weapon? What does all this mean in terms of real life? I know it's real life. It just seems, it seems that nothing is what it seems.

The analyst reasserts what he has been insisting on. The patient doesn't understand him at first. Then again she voices her doubt that any of this has useful meaning for her.

P: The thing I liked so much about all the stuff in [inaudible] house was that none of it was what it was, it was all like, you know, trains made out of, uh, apple wood and little granny dolls with fruit faces and all kinds of things like that. You know everything was transformed—a little, a little lighter [yawn] that was a gun. The other things they were all bigger or smaller and weird. Uh, trudge, trudge. [inaudible] Climbing up the hill to Golgotha carrying a cross on my shoulders. [chuckle] Actually I was first thinking of trudging out of the room.

A: [several inaudible words]—you have to get out of here.

She seems to be toying with ideas. The image of carrying a cross may be related to her masochistic surrender to the situation. He sees her wish to leave as resistance. He has complete confidence in his view of the situation.

P: Sure. I would like to. You know, I mean, I say that I know you're not, you know— first I say that you're making up all of these things. And then I, I mean, I know you're not. But I don't, I haven't the faintest idea of what to do about any of it, you know, so I say that. You know, I don't know what it really means. [pause] I wonder if it's good or bad, though. I feel because of this job that I can't really have it out with J. You know, I can't even decide. I mean, sometimes he seems nice, other times he— I just can't stand him. [pause] Like you, I guess. It's weird to like or not like somebody you never look at.

She makes a connection between J and the analyst. The analyst should consider that the allusion may be that she cannot have it out with him because she needs the therapy. It is also possible that, as this is a recorded analysis, a research analysis, she feels she has made a commitment to a "job" she cannot abandon.

P: [silence] Hmm. I was thinking about a lot of things. And I was thinking I didn't want to tell you any of them, because I wanted to just, you know, deliberately keep it all from you. I was just thinking about whether or not I really hated men. And I was thinking of ones that I don't hate, and I either, either I— if I really like them a lot [yawn] then I feel nervous if I'm around them; if I feel sort of neutral, neutral and positive, toward positive, then that's cool. But there aren't a lot that I really hate. Except I don't know if that's really true. I only hate them some of the times. Like, it's only some things they do that I hate, it's not their whole, whole selves. Every attempt fails. I really want you just to cure me, so I can walk out, you know. I don't want to cure myself, because I don't think I can cure myself.

Her wish to deliberately keep her thoughts from him sounds as though her having been open has only led to a defeat. Her feelings about men have not been clarified, but she realizes she has to have help because she cannot do it herself.

A: And what do you think your idea of a cure is?
P: To not want the cock. To be happy not having one, because I don't have one. And I'm not ever going to have one.

She seems to be parroting what she thinks she is supposed to believe.

A: But you thought of a cure as being, getting one. Being given one. Finding out how to get one.
P: Did I say that? Probably did. Well, either one. It's worse to be left sitting between two stools. Yeah. I guess I really want one and that I'd be— you know, it's like being given Soma, figuring how to live with your infirmity. Just take dope till you die. I guess the real cure would be to figure why I feel I got to have one.
A: Yes.

It sounds as if she is repeating her lesson but is not convinced. Yet the analyst is satisfied that she has seen the light.

P: [shouting] Tell me. [pause] Well, we agree on that. Shit. I really feel [inaudible]. Now how long does it take? When will I know? Why won't you tell me that I will be cured and everything will be all right eventually? But what happens is that I get to the point — and you're right in, like, trying to get me to that point earlier in the hour — because what happens after we get to the point of my saying [shouts], "All right, so it just shows I want a cock again"? That if we can get to that, if I would just come in and say that right off, in the beginning of every hour, then maybe we can move ahead faster, or something. Because what happens is I say that and I get mad and I should really figure out why I want one. Maybe I was born upside down or something. You know, I wish it were, like, just one little thing. Like, it never is, she said, wishing that someone would contradict her. [several inaudible words] It's almost the end. [sigh] [pause] Well, I'm sorry, I've decided I got to leave. It's all over in my head. So I [several inaudible words] get away. So. . .

Her questions about the course of the analysis and her sense that relevant information is being withheld from her lend further support to the hypothesis that the description of J earlier in the hour contained a disguised allusion to the analyst. In particular, just as J keeps her in the dark about the overall scheme of what he is directing (pp. 51–52), so too does the analyst keep her in the dark about the anticipated course of the analysis. In both situations, instead of being brought in as a respected collaborator, she feels she is treated in a demeaning way, as someone who is just supposed to follow orders — whether they make sense to her or not.

A: Oh, tomorrow — can you make it at 10:20 instead of 11:10? Is that OK for you?
P: At 10:20? Yeah. OK. [several inaudible words]
A: So long.

Additional Comments

In the end, the patient sounds despairing. And one can understand why. She has been given an interpretation which she experiences as book learning because it fails to clarify anything for her, except in the most intellectual sense. Yet she is unable to openly declare this dissatisfaction, either because her need is so great or perhaps because the situation provides a hidden masochistic gratification.

Whatever the truth about the role of penis envy in her neurosis, it cannot be gotten at usefully by eliding the transference. The patient experiences the relationship as one in which a tyrannical male forces his will on her without any genuine understanding of what she is feeling. She is left in part submissive and in part raging and distrustful. The analyst fails to see the many plausible clues to the transference which lie in her associations about matters not manifestly about the transference. He also fails to see how his behavior only reinforces how the patient experiences him, and probably strengthens her convictions about what men in general are like. The neurosis has been enacted, not analyzed.

4

PATIENT D: SESSION 69

INTRODUCTION

This session shows an interesting oscillation between a transference and an extra-transference focus. After the therapist ex-
plores an issue outside the transference, the patient introduces
his experience of the relationship by referring to what took place
in a previous session. The therapist could have focused on this
and related it to the earlier data outside the transference. Instead, he at first returns to the extra-transference issue. Eventually, however, he shifts ground and does focus on the interaction the patient brought up from the previous hour. Now it is
the patient who moves away from the transference, although
the therapist brings him back. The patient then defends himself
against the interpretation by saying it is true primarily outside
the transference. In response, the therapist, in the most em-
phatic terms, denies that he is behaving in a way that can plausibly be construed as directive, thereby, ironically, providing
grounds for the very thing he is disclaiming. He reiterates the
transference interpretation but without recognizing how his
own behavior has made the patient's experience plausible. On
the contrary, he reconnects it to the extra-transference situation
and ends by emphasizing an intrapsychic conflict.

THE ANNOTATED SESSION

P: [cough] [pause] There are a few little minor things that I've
noticed, eh, that don't shed any new, new light on what
we've been talking about, but just show the consistent

pattern of, eh, the way my mind works.

The patient begins with a hint of an apology for what he wants to talk about.

P: [cough] The nurse that we've had, eh, leaves Wednesday morning. She was going to leave this weekend, but we had her stay a few more days. Leaves Wednesday morning. And my wife and I view the, her leaving, entirely different-ly. And at least in my viewing it, I can see, is my usual, eh, rose-colored approach; I don't see it—I mean, having the full responsibility of the baby, towards when the nurse is there, I suppose, and when she has the final responsibility —as anything too, eh, eh, too dreadful, let's say, or even too much to worry about. My wife is, is, is worried about how she will act when she has to have the baby all by her-self; and when it cries, if there's something wrong with it, she has to make the [cough] decision, and she has to, to calm it all by herself. Eh, part of the reason that I'm not as worried about it as she is, is that obviously, I'm not there as much of the time as she is, and I think also is very definite-ly my view that things always seem to turn out fine. Eh, I mean, I'm quite certain now that, eh [cough], I'll be able to handle the baby and that she will and so forth. Well, that's about it. I mean, that's all, really, that there is to it. But as I say, I noticed again that it's nothing new, but I, I noticed the consistency of the way I tend to view things.

The apologetic tone continues.

P: [cough] Now, there's another thing that I noticed again. My parents came down [cough] and spent Saturday, eh, Saturday with us. And I made a statement, some time ago, that I was a little surprised at my father's attitude towards our child. Eh [cough], I thought that he didn't seem as in-terested as I had thought he would be, or as I expected he would be, and I wasn't sure what the reason was. I would say that after seeing how he acted this weekend, that my original statement wasn't a true statement of his view, because this weekend he was very excited about the child. And [inaudible]. He's changed his attitude or I misread his first attitude, or perhaps I'm misreading this one, I don't know. [cough] He, he seems quite interested now in, in the child. And he had his movie camera down and was taking pictures of it. And they were—both my mother and father were very, eh, excited and, and interested in it. [cough]

Perhaps his doubt about whether the therapist will be interested in what he has to say parallels his doubt about his father's interest in his child.

P: But there is one thing between my father and me, which took place Friday, of which I want to talk about, because it is a, is a reacting of things that happened before and it seems to put emphasis, in my mind, of the basic relationship between my father and myself—is perhaps unchanging, but just brought to the surface now and again. [cough]

He prefaces whatever he talks about by giving a reason for doing so.

P: Eh, I was driving his car on Friday, doing something for the business. I was out in the afternoon in the car that he owns—that we use in the business a good deal of the time. [cough] I was in R [city], down in the warehouse section there, and was driving behind a truck. Eh, the truck tried to make a right-hand turn, and, eh, he couldn't negotiate the turn. He had to back up and start again. And backing up, he didn't know I was behind him. I honked my horn several times and the truck kept backing up, and finally he hit the car, causing a rather large gash in the front of the truck —in the front of the car, rather. I didn't touch the truck; he had no mark on at all. I hopped out of the car, assuming that he was going to get out of his truck, and we would see what damage was done. And instead the truck just drove off. Eh, I immediately marked down the license number of the truck and thought, well, I was very efficient to have done so. Eh, the gash was not very serious in the front of

the car. And it's— luckily he— was a rather minor repair
job. It's a good-sized gash, but it's only on one piece of met-
al, so that the repair job will not require taking the car
apart too much, and hammering several pieces together.
[cough] Anyway, I was angry at the truck. I felt disappointed at myself for having gotten involved in this, although I felt, absolutely, that I was completely innocent,
because I was standing still, and the truck backed up into
me, in spite of my honking. That's what it amounted to.
And I felt rather pleased. And I felt that I had sort of handled the situation well by getting the license number of the
truck down. I noted the color of the truck, and the type of
truck, and so forth. And I was quite certain that, that, eh,
we could find who owned the truck, and I could— and I, I
thought I had done the best I could in the situation. But
when I got to the office, however, my father, from his questions, I could see hardly—I think—is not sure whether I
had anything to do with this accident or not. The great innocence in my mind, I don't think is in his mind. I think
there is a certain amount of feeling on his part that perhaps
I didn't honk my horn loud enough, for instance—which in
this case, I happen to have done, but in other cases when
I've been in the car with him, I have not always done. And
so I feel, I think that he feels that I didn't honk the horn
loud enough, and that it was, to that extent, my fault. And
second of all, he was very dissatisfied with the amount of
information that I took back with me, as to the, eh, circumstances of the collision. I noted the time and the license
number, and I knew one street on which I was, but I did
not know the name of the other street that formed the corner [inaudible] that I should have written that down,
which I was sure I should have. And I didn't get the, a
good enough description of the truck, he thought. And in
general [cough], I was left with the feeling that I had not
been halfway as efficient as I should have been at that time
and th—— if he would have been there he would have been
much more efficient. Now I say that's a repetition of, eh—I
mean, the upshot of it—as now I have to go to the Motor
Vehicle Bureau and then find out who owns the truck.

[cough] Eh, so the final disposition of the matter is still in the air.

His father was dissatisfied with his performance. The hints of an apology for the subjects he introduces suggest a parallel expectation that the analyst will be dissatisfied with his performance.

P: But the, the thing that seems to me, afterwards—. And I thought that he was unjust and that— not thinking that I had done just the right thing at this time, because I felt that I had done the right thing. This seems to be a repetition of a pattern we always seem to have, where I think that I'm blamed more than I should be, and I'm left with a feeling that, compared with him, I'm relatively inefficient, and he is the great efficient operator. Now part of that I believe is, is, is his feeling that he's more efficient than I am, that he thinks he's more efficient than he actually is. I therefore enjoy it when it turns out that he is not efficient. But partly, eh, I have the feeling, myself, that I am not as in complete control of things as he is, given the same circumstances. I mean, either he's caused me to think that, or I think it for other reasons. But I, I do have that feeling. And then, of course, there's this blame business, which I've seen at other times also; where I thought I've been blamed more than I should have. And the other fact, that it comes to life now, makes me think that probably there [cough]— this is an underlying relationship that we have with each other. And every time we get a set of circumstances that approach this type of set of circumstances, eh, we immediately fall into the sort of pattern that we had time and time again. And I think this shows something basic about our relationship; I'm not sure everything that it shows, but I can see that this pattern keeps reoccurring. I've discussed any number of similar things before in other things, which seem to me to show the, the same attitude; in which— shows a certain antagonism between us. [cough] [pause] And our whole view towards the accident is completely different. I mean I, I, I [cough] considered the gash a rather, eh [cough], easy one to repair. I mean an inexpensive one. Eh, he views it as a large gash and, and a, a difficult one to, to repair. [cough] [silence] I, I, I think that to even broaden [cough] what I said a little bit, I could say that I have the feeling usually that if he's running the operation, things [cough] go well, as far as he's concerned. But when somebody else is running it, there's always something that isn't done right.

A possible allusion in these associations to his experience of the relationship with the analyst may be that he feels he blames himself and is blamed by the analyst more than is warranted for the deficiencies of the analytic work. To follow the parallel further, he may judge the deficiencies to be less serious than what he perceives to be the analyst's view of them. As evidence for the validity of this parallel, the analyst could point to the fact that the patient has not merely been apologizing for his associations but has also argued for their value, as though disagreeing with some anticipated criticism.

P:　I think that's a sort of a broad statement of what I've been saying. I say that because we went out to a restaurant on Saturday evening, and it's a restaurant that M [wife] and I like, and we had a wonderful time. It was, so to speak, the restaurant that we picked out; it was our choice. And he made it a little clear that he wasn't quite satisfied with the service, and it wasn't quite as good as some of the restaurants that he picks out. And it seems to me that I have that feeling all the time about him. [cough] That's not to say that he doesn't compliment me rather highly when I do things right, but I think that that's the exception. But, in general, the feeling is that if he isn't doing the thing, it isn't being done right. And, and as I say, to a certain extent, I have to agree with what he says. It seems to me that if he was at the accident, he may have handled it much more efficiently than I would. I mean, I made the statement earlier—and it was an even more serious statement than this—that I thought that he would make a, a—I'm not sure of what exactly I said. It seems to me that I said something about the fact that I thought that he would make a better father than I would. Did I say something, something like that? That he would make a better grandfather than I would a father, or something of that train, some time ago? And I mean, I felt strongly some time ago about it, although right now I feel —I mean, I enjoy my child so much and, eh, I, I feel that I'm doing a good job as a father, in the very limited time and sense that I can at this time. I feel much more confident with myself as a father right now than I did before the baby was born. [silence]

While it is possible that some comparison of himself with the analyst and some ideas about the analyst's estimate of his own capacities are implicit in these remarks about his father, the evidence seems to warrant only a silent conjecture to that effect.

P: And there's something else that I got sort of a vague feeling about, and I don't know whether I can express it, or whether it's clear in my own mind. And that is a feeling that I've had, it seems to me, part of the time that I don't like to—and I think that's something that may have something directly bearing on this—but I don't like to act in a way that people can anticipate. Eh, let me see if I can make, can make that a little clearer. Eh, I prefer not to, to react in the standard way. Eh, eh, I'm trying to think of some kind of a concrete example. I just have this sort of a vague feeling that at times I, I've desired to react this way when people have, eh, eh, in—I'm trying to make this clear. As I say, it's something I'm not exactly clear on myself. It has something to do with not trying to be, trying not to be just like everybody else.

What seems like a new topic, on the manifest level at least, has been introduced. Although its connection with what went before is not entirely clear, the nonconformist, rebellious attitude (expressed with difficulty here) would certainly conflict with any inclination the patient may have to comply with either the father's or the analyst's expectations. In retrospect, one could say that while he may be concerned about displeasing the analyst, the patient is even more averse to merely doing what he takes to be the analyst's bidding.

P: But in more— specifically I, I can recall vaguely the feeling of that when people have said to me, "Oh, eh, don't you think this is cute?" or "This is nice," and everybody else has said that this is nice, I have the feeling of not wanting to, to say that; not wanting to, to react in the way that everybody expects me to act, that everyone before me has acted. I remember in college being given a — in the psychology courses that we had — various tests and reaction tests, and so forth — trying not to make the reaction that was anticipated by everybody. I, I don't think it was just trying to be stubborn about it. I think that there was some more important feeling involved in that. But, as I say, it's not all clear to me exactly what the feeling is. [pause] I remember that we were, we were shown a TAT card and a picture on it. [cough] And the picture, I believe, was a [cough], a nude woman, lying on a bed — something like that. And I remember, in this particular instance, I realized that probably the reaction that everybody would have would be some kind of a story dealing with a nude woman, or sex of some sort. But I had a very strong feeling that I wanted to [cough], not to react as everyone reacted. And then — in the particular instance, it was quite clear in my mind — and so I gave a reaction that was quite foreign to the story. It only dram——, it only dragged the picture in on a very oblique sort of a way. I remember that particular instance. I don't remember too many instances when this is actually demonstrated but I, I just am aware of that, that feeling.

A: What did you react? What did you say?

The central issue seems to be the patient's having avoided saying the expected rather than what he actually did say, but the analyst may feel that with more information about the episode he will be able to understand it better. It may also be noted that although the manifest theme is the patient's oppositional tendency, he may be responding covertly to what he believes is the analyst's interest in sex.

P: Eh, I don't remember the, the story very well. I mean it was, eh, it's so many years ago. But I recall I told a story about a friend of mine. Eh, I don't remember any of the details, eh, at all, except that I, I, I attached, I, I tied it up with the picture in that I said that this was a, a—he was saying goodbye to this girl at this time, leaving, going out the door; I don't remember whether it was a door in the picture, or not. Eh, my friend was saying goodbye to this woman, who was his mistress at the time. I think this was, eh, leaving out the door—something like that. The story had very little to do with this, however. It really was an involved story about this boy.

A: But the story, but the picture obviously, of course, was about a nude woman.

P: Yes.

A: And yet you tried to be different and make it into a story about a boy?

P: Yes.

A: In other words, about somebody who really isn't part of the original picture?

P: Yes.

A: Why?

P: Well, I would say now, eh, I would, I would—I think that it has a lot to do with what I was just telling you. That I, I would say beyond that, eh, at that time, eh, I—. No. I would say this: that, that apparently, I mean, it's obvious to me now that I have a tremendous amount of inhibitions about sex, and I would assume that it has something to do with that. That I didn't want to, to discuss the, the nude woman, I suppose. I mean, I don't really know.

There is some ambiguity here about whether the analyst is interested in exploring the patient's general dislike of doing the expected or some specific hang-up about sex. Needless to say, the two may be related and could be fruitfully explored together. At this point, however, there is a danger that the therapist may get caught up in the specific implications of the particular memory that the patient has reported, thereby losing sight of the manifest train of thought concerning the patient's feelings in his relationship with his father, as well as overlooking the latent issues in the analytic relationship. The very fact that the analyst speaks now, for the first time, suggests a selective interest in manifestly sexual themes and the possibility of a subtle imposition of this preference on the patient.

A: You suppose?
P: I beg your pardon?
A: I say, "You suppose?"
P: Yes. I mean, that would seem to me. . .
A: Do you have to suppose?
P: [laughing] I don't know, but I don't like to say anything too definite, and maybe. . .
A: Why not? Why not?
P: Well, because I don't know. I, I'd say, yes; I, it just seems to me that that's probably what it was.
A: And if you were the psychologist evaluating your responses to this test situation, eh, what then would you say? How would you comment on this reaction to this card?
P: Well, of course, the interesting thing is— and [cough] probably I was trying not to react in the, in the typical manner. Probably it wouldn't take too much of a trained psychologist to interpret that for what it was.
A: But, indeed, you're not even a trained psychologist.
P: And I've interpreted it.
A: And can [laughing] interpret it.
P: That's right.
A: That the evasion—one might say, put it that way—even, evasion of responding to the direct material in itself, is equally significant.
P: Yes, I, I, I'm quite positive that it is. It certainly is significant.
A: You see the reason that you advance—"I want to be different"—well, it may be so. I mean, I don't question that reason. But obviously the underlying reason is much more important than the superficial one.

The analyst seems to be hectoring the patient a bit. Furthermore, he is pushing his own convictions about what is underlying and what is superficial, about what is important and what is not. Will he not be experienced as knowing better than the patient, i.e., as the patient experiences his father?

P: Yes. I certainly say. Well, definitely in, in that case. Probably. Although I, I say that I, I, I still have this vague feeling that maybe, maybe this vague feeling is only a conglomeration of feelings that have to do with the results of my inhibitions, and that may very well be, as a result of this instance, and many other instances in which I was conscious of my inhibitions preventing me from giving a completely free answer. Maybe that's the— and maybe some of that may be this, may be this vague feeling I have of attempting to act differently.

The patient returns to the possible importance of his presenting feeling, albeit diffidently and vaguely, presumably because he is disagreeing somewhat with the analyst's evaluation of what is superficial and what is deep.

A: Now, if you were in a test situation of that sort, the psychologist would then go over the cards with you and ask you: "Why did you say that?"—as, indeed, I have just asked you.

P: Yes.

A: And so, a second response would be elicited: "Well, I suppose it is an inhibition about sex." And the psychologist, as I am, would then become aware that there is a second important factor in your response. To quote you: "I don't like to say anything too definite." Since I am not a psychologist here and the test results, one might say, are entirely for my own purposes, you know...

P: Hmm.

A: You're the guinea pig, and not supposed to know anything about the results. Since I am not a psychologist, the situation is different. I present to you, here is a second point in your response which is as equally significant as the first: "I don't like to say anything too definite."

Now the analyst does seem to be attaching importance to the patient's presenting feeling.

P: Well, what about that one now? I see the significance of the first; I mean, that's very clear in my mind now. I don't see the significance of the second.

A: Well, I ask you, indeed, of course, to consider.

P: You mean specifically, as concerns sex, or in general, as it concerns more things than that?

A: Specifically as concerns sex, yes. Because that is the connection in which you made that statement. But now that you mention it, one could, I think, ask perhaps: Is not that "I don't like to say anything too definite" also applicable to other fields of thought, feeling? In other words, is that not, perhaps, a rather general characteristic of you?

The interaction is interesting. The patient isn't sure whether the analyst is focusing on sex or not. When he asks, it becomes clear that the analyst meant sex, but the question the patient asked apparently made the analyst realize it might indeed be useful to broaden the issue to a character trait.

P: Well, that I don't know. That, that's what I ask you: in which way you mean it.

A: I take this statement on its face value at this point.

P: [cough] [pause] Well, what does the indefiniteness mean? Can you say that?

A: Can you?

P: Well, it obviously means indecision, eh, but, beyond that, I don't know what that means. [cough] I mean, I'd say that, at that time that my, my meaning of that particular instance that you picked up in the sentence, eh, had, had this in, in back of it, and that is, that at many junctions, as we go along, I don't exactly have in mind what you have in mind. And you ask me something, and — to take an example from last time, which is fresh in my mind — I believe it was last time, or the time before — I was discussing this dream, and, eh, I was discussing in whose eyes the feeling was to be, and you said, "Well, in whose eyes?" And I said, "In mine, or in my father's," and you said, "No, no, no," that it was in yours. And, I mean, that sort of demonstrates that what I have in mind, I don't like to say anything too sure about it, till I find out that's what you're driving at, or whether you're driving at something else entirely different.

It now becomes clear that when the patient said he does not like to say anything too definite (p. 78), he was alluding to his experience of the relationship, in which he attempts to divine what the analyst has in mind. In order to avoid saying something that might conflict with what the analyst has in mind, he tries not to say anything too definite.

What makes this point clear is that the patient turns explicitly to the analytic interaction and refers to an exchange in the preceding hour. From his account, one can deduce that the therapist had some particular conviction he was conveying to the patient, that the patient misunderstood him, and that the therapist somewhat impatiently — "No, no, no" — corrected the patient, or at least that was how the patient experienced it. This is the kind of exchange that the patient attempts to avoid by not saying anything too definite. The account bears out the earlier suggestion that the patient experiences the analytic interaction as similar to what goes on with his father. He feels criticized by someone who considers that he can do things better.

What is especially noteworthy from the point of view of technique is that it is the patient who turns to his experience of the relationship, however partially, and his doing so illuminates the interactive implication of his saying he doesn't like to say anything too definite. It would be desirable for the analyst to pick up on this implication and encourage the patient to expand on how he experienced the earlier exchange.

A: That sounds perhaps quite reasonable in that situation.
P: Well, that's what I thought.
A: But after all that was my statement, not yours. That the figure, the figures represented myself.
P: Yes.
A: But it fits as a general characteristic. It has the obvious implication that you never come to any clear-cut decisions, that none of your opinions and beliefs and feelings are definitely this and not that. Because if you look a moment, I think you will see that this is quite intimately related to the

tendency to put a nice, rosy finish to the surface of things.

The analyst does not focus on the patient's experience in the episode, except, at first, to say it sounds reasonable. Yet in a moment he is criticizing the patient for the character trait. The opportunity has been lost for seeing how, from the patient's point of view, it is better for him to avoid saying anything too definite lest he collide with and be humiliated by the one who knows better.

P: In what way is that connected?

A: Well, what do you think?

P: Well, I don't see why a rosy [cough] finish on things can't go with definite decisions as well as indefinite ones. Really, I mean, I don't see why you can't make a decision and, and act on it, and be very certain that everything is fine, if that was the right decision to make.

A: Is it true in real life that every decision, and the activity resulting from the decision, indicates a rosy picture?

P: No. All decisions are not right, obviously.

A: Not only not all decisions are not right, but many decisions may be arrived at only with extreme difficulty.

P: Yes.

A: But the implication—"I don't like to say anything too definite"—is more closely associated with the indecisiveness in which, which the rosy surface hides. Everything appears well and good and clear on the surface, but perhaps not quite so clear beneath the surface.

P: I see. Uh-huh.

One may doubt that the patient has indeed been convinced by this argument.

A: "Everything is fine. I know where I'm going. I've made up my mind."

P: Well, you say, in fact, then I'm quite indecisive. Is that right? Is that what you're saying?

A: Could—your statement "I don't like to say anything too definite," I think, means precisely that.

P: Well, would you say there was particular evidence for that
      in what I said before? I mean, that hasn't particularly
      struck me about myself as other things have.

The basic fault in the therapist's approach is exposed. The patient is not persuaded that indecisiveness is in fact a prominent
feature of his behavior. What would have made the discussion
meaningful and persuasive would have been an examination of
his experience in the episode he described. It would have brought
out an understandable explanation for his dislike of saying anything too definite. A more subtle and immediate example of his
aversion to risking a confrontation in which he will be put down
is the above debate over the connection between decisiveness
and rosy outlooks. Although he concedes defeat, it is not convincing to us.

A: But I think if you look particularly at your behavior here, I
      think that is quite prominent. The indecisiveness of what
      you do here. You see, one has to be very careful. You al-
      lude to an example of the last hour: I say something. You
      are not fully convinced that my interpretation is correct,
      but that sounds quite logical and reasonable. But what do
      you do at that point, or from that point on? Not only allud-
      ing to this example of yesterday's hour, but many times be-
      fore...
P: What do I do?
A: Yeah.
P: I don't know. I mean, you explain something; I don't agree
      with you, completely. Well, I think eventually I take over
      your, your, your analysis, it seems to me. Isn't that what
      you have in mind?
A: If, indeed, you do that, then whose decision?
P: It was your decision, actually.
A: My decision. And you, inside of yourself, can always make
      mental reservations: "Well, after all, this isn't what I've de-
      cided. He's decided that. And since I am not sure, that I
      have doubts, I can always reserve to myself the opportu-
      nity of withdrawing my agreement."

The analyst does return to the episode of the previous hour. But he does not examine the patient's experience in detail, and he certainly pays no attention to how the patient may have felt the analyst's behavior justified his own reluctance to say anything "too definite." Instead, he argues for his own view in a way which may very well be experienced by the patient as an attempt to impose it on the patient. Furthermore, the analyst proceeds to explain how the patient uses his alleged indecision in the interaction. In fact, the analyst has yet to fashion a solid basis for such a contention.

P: [cough] Well, I'll say one thing, that I do— and it seems to me to point to indecision, although—or—I frankly say that it's not something that I have associated with myself, certainly consciously. I mean, I haven't really been aware of it until now that you talk about it—but I would say this that tends to bear that out—and that is, my avoiding sharp breaks with people, sharp fights, and so forth. There is a tendency there to, to drift with the status quo.

Here the patient does concede something that may "point to indecision" in his "avoiding sharp breaks" with people. Indeed, at the moment he is probably avoiding a sharp break with the analyst by accommodating to his opinion. The interaction is probably similar to that with his father, where, despite the antagonism (p. 73, line 34), he avoids a sharp break.

In fact, the patient's reflections here could be regarded as a tactful attempt on his part to finally get back to the issue he was implicitly struggling with earlier in the hour: the conflict between compliance and assertion of individuality. This issue, which the patient illustrated with his memory of his response to the TAT (p. 76), has gotten lost precisely because the therapist imposed his observation of the patient's indecisiveness just when the patient was speaking of his resolve to be different and to do the opposite of what he thought was expected of him. The other side of the conflict, stated now, is the tendency "to drift with the status quo." Perhaps, the conflict as a whole results in indecision or indefiniteness—an assertiveness that is half-negated by disclaimers and apologies.

A: All right.

P: Which is obviously indecision.
A: Which is, I think, what you have already spoken about.
P: Yes.
A: Rather than come to a sharp, decisive fight, conflict; it is better, then, to accept my opinion, my decision, and let things drift along in that way.

This statement of the patient's experience of the relationship is especially to be commended because it returns the patient's general discussion explicitly to the patient-analyst interaction. Its defect is that the interaction is described generally rather than tied to a specific and immediate event. Moreover, in the very act of persuading the patient that the analyst's point of view is correct, the analyst is probably experienced by the patient as imposing this view. The patient probably feels he must assent in order to avoid a "sharp break." Ironically, the analyst, even while seemingly trying to promote the patient's autonomy, may be experienced as domineering.

Since the analyst seems right at this point, however, it is doubtful that the patient feels pushed in the same way that he felt pushed earlier, when the analyst was wider of the mark. The issue is more subtle now because the analyst's point of view is probably the same as the patient's. Nevertheless, he may still feel he is knuckling under when he agrees with what the analyst says.

P: That is, that's, that's, that's probably right; although, there is more to it, as far as this is concerned, than there is as far as other things are concerned, it seems to me. I mean, I think that I would be a damn fool if I spent a lot of time arguing with you and your interpretations on various things that I do. Not only would I waste time, but it, it would be a very, eh, wa——, unfair type of an argument, because I would be using prejudice against presumably your knowledge, which would seem to me to—I mean, I don't think I'm in as strong [inaudible] here not to ta——. I think I'm more right here in the abstract sense to take your view than I am outside, where a sharp break with my father, or with the people I work with, or in other situations, is more an even thing. Where I'm more confident to be the judge, it seems to me. I mean, I see what you mean, but I don't think, I, I, I can't see what's something indecisive here in taking what you think. I think it's much more so outside.

This is a common cliché rationalization for the patient's deference to the analyst's authority. It's a transparent resistance to an aspect of the patient's experience of the relationship that is likely to occur no matter how good the therapist's technique is. At the same time the patient's resistance probably would have been lessened had the analyst focused more sharply and thoroughly on the patient's experience of the relationship, including examining how the patient felt his attitude was a necessary self-protection. Incidentally, the patient's remark, while seeming to accept the analyst's authority, is at the same time a subtle defiance of this authority, since he is rejecting the analyst's interpretation (p. 85, lines 4–6).

A: But after all, my interpretations are not offered to you in the nature of decisions: "This you must accept."
P: Yes, I understand.
A: They are, they are offered to you, really, for you to consider, and for you to make up your own mind about. But taking my interpretations as a decision—"This is right"—simply avoids, therefore, the necessity of you having to do any further thinking about it.
P: That, that, that's probably true, I guess.

The analyst affirms his good intentions, and his remark does have the merit of keeping the focus on the patient's compliance. But it ignores the reasons the patient has for disbelieving him: for example, it ignores the fact that in the key episode spontaneously brought up by the patient, he experienced the analyst not as allowing him to make up his own mind but as imposing a view on him. Furthermore, with the clear vision of hindsight, one can see that the patient may be offended at being told that he seeks to avoid any "further thinking." His response—"that's probably true, I guess"—exemplifies the pseudo-compliance we noted earlier. The ideal interpretation would have included reference to the pseudo-compliance, as well as to anything in the analyst's behavior that the patient experienced as coercive, even if only intended as of gentle pressure.

A: You can drift along: "I don't have to struggle through these doubts of mine — the lack of clarity, the lack of factual information that is necessary in order to make my own decision. I can simply accept his, and let things drift along."

P: That's what you mean by my indecisive behavior here?

A: That is what the indecisive behavior would result in — drifting.

P: Yes.

A: Nothing ever becomes crystal clear. Nothing ever becomes sharp and definitive: it is this, and not anything else. It is as if, therefore, the analysis becomes something which has a very familiar ring to it, of having decisions imposed upon you, which you superficially accept, and, inwardly, have many reservations about. In other words, one might say, rather than an open conflict, you handle the situation in a much more subtle fashion; you sabotage it without the slightest appearance of overt conflict.

P: Well, I, I, I still say that it seems to me that — I don't know. The mental reservations are not always so strong, it seems to me, and, and interpretations that you've made on a lot of things, it seems to me, that I agree on a lot of things.

The analyst's final interpretation above is logical and clear and now includes the element of pseudo-compliance which amounts to sabotage. The patient continues to resist, though his response is an indirect confirmation: "not always so strong" implies sometimes strong reservations and "a lot of things" indicates not everything. In assessing this reaction, one can emphasize either that such resistance is inevitable or that it might be somewhat diminished by further exploring the pseudo-compliance in the patient's very response to the interpretation of pseudo-compliance, including examining what in the manner of the analyst persuades the patient (however unconsciously) that a pseudo-compliant response is necessary.

A: Well, let us say that they're not so conscious — your mental reservations.

P: That, that, that may be so. Although, if I say I don't know here, that, that, that's the truth.

A: Because, you see, the interesting thing is that you drift, therefore, or manipulate the situation here, so that it directly parallels a very familiar situation to you: your father says something, and it is up to you to either take his decision, or, if you don't, to come in open conflict with him. There, the best thing to do [inaudible] accept his decision and to have mental reservations about it.

P: That . . .

A: Your father says—in any way—openly, or in a less open way—your antipathies are not so innocent. And I'm not referring to this accident, but to things which are much more profound, in which the word "innocent" came up. "This red mark on my neck means nothing bad or wrong: I am entirely innocent." Your father thinks differently. There is no open conflict, but you, inside of yourself, drift along because you have never made up your own mind as to whether the act was really innocent or not. Because it is obvious, from things that you have said recently, that you are not at all convinced as to your innocence.

The analyst makes a concession to the resistance by noting the reservations are not so conscious, but the patient's equivocation continues. The subsequent parallel the analyst draws to the patient's interaction with his father is clear and cogent, although it has the disadvantage of drawing attention away from the immediate interaction. The patient then starts to say something but is interrupted by the analyst, who goes on to refer to some earlier content which is clearly important. Still, this very interaction suggests a basis for the patient's experience of the analyst as pressing his convictions in a way that shuts off any significant opposition.

P: In a, in a, in a general way, yes.

A: And quite specifically, coming back to this TAT picture, one might say that you give your innocence away by even avoiding completely saying anything about the nude woman. You're not a psychologist, but you could easily question, "Well, why does this test patient avoid the card? What is he hiding?"

P: Yes. Well, that's, that's, well, I say that, that's obvious now.

A: All right. We'll stop today.

P: OK. See you Wednesday.

A: Goodbye.

ADDITIONAL COMMENTS

It is possible that the analyst's ending the hour with the specific sexual reference betrays a predetermined agenda. Nevertheless, during most of the session he has focused on the patient's interpersonal attitudes of pseudo-compliance and rebellion, which are, in this session at least, more directly of concern to the patient. Despite an inauspicious beginning, the analyst does pretty well overall. The session, however, does illustrate a significant and common flaw — the enactment, in the process, of the content of the interpretation without an interpretation of this enactment. At the end the patient agrees: "that's obvious now." But that agreement may very well represent the same pseudo-compliance.

The patient probably experiences the session as a repetition of the struggle with his father. Once again he has lost, although perhaps with some glimmering of how the struggle takes place and what his role is. Were the technique better, the analyst would interpret the immediate interaction more. Here we do not mean to imply that had he done so, the resistance would simply have melted away. It is clearly formidable. Nor can we blame the analyst for being seduced into repeating, however mildly, the father's role. What one would hope is that he will become aware of this and enact it to a lesser degree, while progressively bringing the immediate interaction into his interpretations.

5

PATIENT E: SESSION 93

INTRODUCTION

This session is a good example of the explication of important
issues in the transference as a result of the analyst's exploration
of the meaning of an overt event in the therapy—in this instance,
the patient's cancellation of an appointment. The patient responds to the analyst's pursuit of some manifest meanings of the
cancellation by revealing that he experiences the pursuit itself as
having homosexual implications. The analyst follows up with a
commendable recognition of how his own behavior is being
plausibly experienced by the patient as betraying homosexuality. At the same time the manner in which he makes these interpretations continues to be plausibly experienced by the patient
as having homosexual implications, suggesting that the analyst
is only partially aware of them. The session thus illustrates the
very common phenomenon of the enactment in interpretation
of the very issue which is being interpreted. More precisely, in
this instance, what is being enacted is considered to be an indirect expression of what is being interpreted, since what is being
interpreted is homosexuality, while what is being enacted is
dominance and submission.

The session also clearly illustrates the discomfort of an analyst who is overtly interacting with his patient in a way which
his training has prohibited. We anticipate that this will be a
common experience of analysts with traditional training who attempt to employ the technique we are advocating, since our
technique tends to lead to a freer kind of interaction with the patient. In turn, a patient with some knowledge of accepted analytic practice is likely to ascribe such discomfort to an analyst

91

who is more interactive than the patient expects. For an illustration, see Lipton's (1977) vignette about his offering his patient a thermometer to take her temperature when he thought she was ill.

The Annotated Session

P: Good morning.

A: Hi.

P: [pause] Well—I really can't tell you why I didn't come yesterday. Like, uh, I had every intention of coming but then, uh, this guy at school said, "Hey, you want to go out for a ride in my boat," you know, and I said, "All right," and, uh —'cause it was a real nice day out yesterday—about 70, 75 —at least, it felt like it. And, uh, so he was ready to go at 11, you know, and I said, "No, I can't make it until 12:30," you know. And he said, "Oh, yeah. 'Cause you gotta go down to the shrink." And I goes, "Yeah." I said, "But I might cut the shrink today," and he says, "Well, if you cut, come on over, I'll be waiting for you." So I did. And—I don't know. I thought about calling and then I said, "Naw, I won't call." Uh, I figured, you know, it'd be—. Well, it'd be like, you know, I was gonna do it deliberately, you know; if I didn't call I might give you the impression that— aw, "I just can't come today," you know, "it's just too much," you know. So I thought: "I'll give him that impression and I won't call." [pause]

The patient refers explicitly to an event in the transference which would universally be considered important to explore. As described in Volume I, resistance to the awareness of transference can be divided into resistance to awareness that something has transference meaning and resistance to awareness of what that meaning is. Here the latter is the issue. While the patient realizes that what he has done has to do with his feelings about the therapist, it seems likely that there is much to learn about what those feelings are.

A: I want to be sure I understand that. You mean, if you didn't call, then I would assume that it was not deliberate.

This seems to be a useful clarification.

P: Yeah. Right. You know, I said, "Aw, I just can't help it," you know.
A: But you obviously knew that when you came you would tell me it was deliberate so I would know.
P: Yeah. But, uh, at least here I could assess your reaction, you know. Nil anyway. [laughs] But, at least, I wouldn't wonder about it, you know. I didn't want to worry about — oh, you know, "What are you thinking now?" you know.
A: So what's your assessment?
P: Oh, I don't know. I don't know if I was assessing or just I didn't want to worry about it for the day.
A: No. I mean today.
P: Oh. I don't know. I didn't, I got the impression already you didn't think it was any big thing, you know. I mean you weren't pissed off or anything when I came in, you know.
A: What gave you that impression?
P: Just —. Well, maybe that's the impression I want to see.
A: Oh.
P: Seemed like nothing had changed or . . .
A: "Well, I was so terribly relieved. You hadn't come yesterday and you were late today; I thought you were never coming anymore." [patient laughs]

The therapist is speculating on the attitude the patient may attribute to him. He may well be drawing on his actual countertransference as a basis for his speculation, that is, he guesses that the patient may have attributed something to him that he actually has experienced. This might, therefore, be an example of using the countertransference to formulate an interpretation, without, however, confessing the nature of the countertransference. The interpretation is marred by the joking manner in which it is offered. By caricaturing the patient's idea about the therapist's experience ("I was so terribly relieved"), the therapist seems, in effect, to mock it instead of granting it plausibility.

P: Aaw—you'd have to give me at least a week—before you'd
    start thinking that. [pause] At least, that's my reasoning
    anyway.

The flip manner in which the interpretation was offered may
have invited this somewhat flip response.

A: In any case, you didn't feel that my greeting indicated I
    was pissed off, huh?
P: No. No. Or your manner, so far. [pause] I don't know. It's
    just all these—well, I don't know how to describe them. I
    just get tired of feeling, you know—or being constantly re-
    minded, you know, that I'm fucked up, you know. It'd be
    nice if I could just hide, you know, and say, "I'm all right
    and everybody else is wrong."
A: Was there anything about Monday's hour that you think
    played any role in your deciding to skip Tuesday?

The patient here makes an important statement about his experience of the therapy. The therapist would do well to focus on
that directly. His purpose might be better served, for example,
if he asked whether anything that occurred Monday contributed to the specific feeling about therapy the patient has just described. Still, his question does direct the patient's attention to
the covert precipitants of his current attitude.

P: I don't know. I came away with Monday, from Monday,
    with the impression that I had talked a lot, you know, and
    that, uh, I had been glad to see you back, you know, and I
    realized what effect your going away had on me. Not what
    effect but degree, you know, that your going away affected
    me. And, you know, I started getting all these thoughts
    about—oh Jesus, you know—I shouldn't become attached
    to you. You're not a real person. I should become attached
    to somebody else or something else or [sigh]. And it seemed
    to be a very dependent type of feeling. . .

A: Yeah. That was the idea I had in mind. [pause] Do you
    follow?

The therapist's question has borne fruit. The patient's feeling of
dependency may have been increased by his friend's taunt
about having to see his shrink. It should be noted, however, that
the therapist's comment that he had anticipated the patient's
response may be experienced by the patient as controlling. The
analyst should be alert for this.

P: Yeah. Yeah. And I want to assert my independence — shit,
    you know — even to the point where I'll say, "Fuck you, I
    ain't coming at all."
A: Yeah. I think Monday was, Monday was too much, so you
    cancelled it out by not coming Tuesday. At least, that seems
    to me to be a real possibility. That you had admitted and,
    perhaps, even felt a degree of attachment that, uh, just
    seemed too dangerous, frightening — whatever the hell
    word you want to use for it. So, as I say, you wiped that
    out by not coming Tuesday, in case I started getting the
    wrong idea. [laugh]

Collaboratively, the analyst and patient seem to have arrived at
a cogent explanation for the missed appointment. The therapist, however, goes a little beyond what the evidence would
seem to support when he introduces the notion of his getting the
"wrong idea." Also, the analyst's laughter and his somewhat
cavalier attitude may diminish the chances for a sober examination of what is clearly a very serious issue for the patient.

P: Yeah. I also came away with the impression that I didn't
    really say very much Monday compared to what I wanted
    to say, but I didn't know what I wanted to say. You know,
    like, I had all these feelings, you know, and everything
    when you were gone, you know, about other people and
    other things, and I was active and I pretty much blotted
    them out, you know. Like, I can't even remember now. I
    can remember thinking, you know, through the course of
    last week — "Aw, gee, I'll have to remember to relate this" —

"I'll have to remember to relate this and I'll have to remember to relate how I felt here," and [sigh], but I can't remember what now. It almost seemed as if I'd gotten back in the groove so easily, you know. Like, uh, well, I'm gonna study some more again, you know. I'm gonna, you know, go down to you every day and...

A: I'm not quite clear. You got back in the groove after I came back or while I was away?

P: After you came back, you know.

A: You mean, your behavior the week I was away, you think, was different?

P: [sigh] My attitudes were— yeah, you know.

A: In what way?

P: I felt as if each day I had to make a separate decision about —"Wow, what am I gonna do today?" you know—"What am I not gonna do and how am I gonna approach today?" And when you came back, it seemed like they were all made for me, you know, as if I said, "Well, gotta get back on the old schedule there, you know, and go to the shrink, you know, and he expects some kind of improvement or..." [?] "Go to work and be industrious and go to school and study hard in between and don't fuck off and get back on my diet and," you know...

A: So apparently when I'm away you feel thrown on your own responsibility.

Yes, but the therapist would do well here to inquire further into the complex feelings the patient had while he was gone. The patient had to make his own decisions but he may have derived some pleasure from that in contrast to the irksome dependent and compliant role he feels obliged to assume in the analysis.

P: Yeah. Right.

A: That I understand, but it also sounds— I was trying to understand what it meant that you thought of these various things: "I have to tell him, I have to tell him this, that, and the other," and then they're all gone. I wondered if you actually behaved any differently too. And if that— I mean, these things you were gonna tell, whether they indicate that.

P: I don't know. It seemed like I was feeling more.

A: That's what I thought you implied.

P: Yeah. Mostly, I think, in the general direction of depress-
    ing, or frustration, or whatever, you know.

A: I was wondering if there was some connection between,
    uh, your forgetting and the idea that—I don't know how to
    put it exactly—but if something happened and you said,
    "Gee, I have to remember to tell him this," that suggests I
    was in your thoughts and, again, means something to you,
    and maybe, again, the forgetting is an effort to block that
    out.

Here, too, the interpretation might be more complete if it included a reference to the satisfaction the patient felt at being his
own man while the therapist was away and his dismay about
losing that feeling when the therapist returned. At the same
time, it must be admitted that the patient's remarks are somewhat obscure and the therapist might have done better to con-
fine himself to asking the patient to clarify what he was saying.

P: Yeah. Right. 'Cause you know, most of the situations—at
    least I get the feeling that they were— well, "I'll tell you
    that and it'll be all right again," or "At least, somebody'll
    understand what's going on"—"At least, somebody will see
    my point of view," you know. Or: "They won't th-think I'm
    foolish for expressing these feelings." You won't anyway—
    as opposed to other people. [sigh] [pause of 55 seconds]

A: Why did that stop you?

The sigh and the pause suggest that something about the directly positive feelings just expressed may be inhibiting the patient
from going on.

P: No. Just something popped in my mind and I don't know
    if I should relate it to you or not. [analyst laughs] You
    know, I'm gonna anyway but I don't want to.

A: So you have to struggle with whether— you mean, the si-
    lence is an effort to make yourself do it?

P: Yeah.

A: Or was it maybe designed to. . .

P: Well, to present it in a way that it would be pal-palatable to me and, you know. . .

A: I thought maybe you were waiting long enough for me to say something so that when you speak, it's sort of 'cause I'm making you.

The therapist is trying to make explicit every nuance of the relationship, but what is his basis for this interpretation? Perhaps it is a dim recognition that for the patient the requirement to speak his thoughts may carry a disturbing sense of being coerced just as he may have felt that his attending sessions regularly was in response to an implicit demand by the therapist. But rather than introduce what is speculation at this point — that the patient wants to create the impression that he is being coerced — the analyst would do better to empathize with the patient's more conscious struggle against complying with the analyst's expectation.

P: Well, I kinda realized that a little way into it, you know, but then I said — "Aw, well, I better get something said," you know, and then I was — so anyway — . No. I don't think you were trying to — the idea of you coaxing me didn't come along until just before you opened your mouth. [sigh] [pause] And for a minute there, you know, I heard me try to say — well, I didn't think of anything, you know, but that's not true. No. I was thinking about this thing I did yesterday — riding in the boat with this other guy — and, uh, the fact that, you know, and this probably, incidentally, has some bearing on our relationship. . .

The patient does confirm the interpretation, at least by affirmation. It is noteworthy that he himself makes explicit that what he is about to tell has some bearing on the relationship with the analyst. He is aware that what is not manifestly about the transference may nevertheless allude to it.

A: Incidentally, what?

P: Uh. . .

A: You said that so fast.

P: Has some bearing on our relationship, I think.

A: Oh.

P: I don't know. I ran into him—he was in one of my classes and I really dig this guy as a friend 'cause he's my age and he's the only guy in the whole school, so far, that I've run into that thinks like I do, you know. Not one of these goofy kids that I can't relate to. But, but anyway, whenever I'm around him, you know, I wonder, you know, about my actions and how he's gonna interpret them—like, is he gonna think I'm a faggot or something like that 'cause I prefer his company over that of all these fine-ass broads in the school, you know? Which I do, you know. I mean, I'll sit there and look at these broads and I'll say: "Aw, Jesus, what am I gonna say to them?" They won't say nothing, you know. So—. But I can't seem to express any positive feelings or any, like— enjoyment, you know, without wondering, you know: Is this guy gonna think I'm a faggot, you know? And before I voiced those words—I never applied them here—but I'm sure the same thing goes on here, you know. [pause] Uh. [slight pause] I don't know if it's— yeah, part of it is, you know, I wonder if I express positive feelings toward you, if you'll think there's some over—, sexual overtones there, you know. I mean, that's the first thought that hits me and quickly, you know, I'll follow it up by, uh—oh, what was I gonna say? —like, you know, it's not a manly thing to do, you know—express affection or all this shit and enjoyment and enthusiasm, you know. You're supposed to be cool and stay casual and that's it.

The connection between this and what preceded the silence now becomes clear, since before the silence he expressed positive feelings to the therapist. The therapist has probably facilitated the patient's rich explication of his experience of the relationship through the careful and systematic inquiries and interpretive work.

A: Did this start with some recollection of some specific, concrete something-or-other you felt or said or did? — with him?

It does not seem timely at this point to depart from the transference issue the patient has raised, although the analyst's interest in what actually happened on the boat is understandable and may ultimately reflect on the transference.

P: No. The immediate thought that flashed into my head — no, not really — the thought that flashed into my head —. What were we talking about before I stopped talking?

A: I think, if I remember correctly, I made an interpretation to the effect that, uh, your forgetting the things you were going to tell me had something to do with the fact when you get such a thought — "Gee, I have to tell him this" — that meant you were thinking about me and cared about me.

It is possible that this interaction was a subtle request by the patient to be directed, with which the analyst complied without realizing what was being enacted.

P: Yeah. Right. And. . .

A: And I suppose that's what led to your thinking: "Oh, my God, if I admit that then he'll think I'm a faggot"?

P: Yeah. Well, the thought that flashed into my head was, uh, an image of this guy tellin' me, "Hey, man, I'm a faggot," and then me saying, "Oh, what a relief, all the time I thought I was having, you know, homosexual leanings, you know, because I'm uptight about the whole subject, you know, and that's a big load off my mind, you know, that you're the one that caused this charged atmosphere and not me." [laugh] [pause] That was the thought that just entered my head, you know, and then after that came the silence and I was trying to think about what it meant. [pause] It's almost as if I'm saying to you: "Hey, doc, you're the one that's fucked up and I'm sane, you know, and you're the one that's making me wonder about it."

A: Yes. And I — maybe even more, uh, explicitly. My interpretation that you care about me meant to you that I was saying that I'm a faggot.

The therapist insists on drawing the parallel more directly between himself and the man on the boat and does not allow the patient to evade this connection by substituting "insane" for "faggot" when speaking of the therapist. Perhaps, it would have been better if he had followed this up with an open-ended question regarding the basis for the patient's impression instead of proposing a basis himself.

Incidentally, if the patient had not spontaneously made the connection between the man on the boat and the therapist, it would have been appropriate for the therapist to do so. It is this kind of interpretation that both the therapist and the patient often avoid because of its disparagement of the therapist.

P: Yeah.
A: As if the reason I make such an interpretation or think about it is because I care.
P: Yeah. You want me to care. Right.
A: So I want you to 'cause I'm homosexually attracted to you.
P: [pause] Well, sexually attracted.
A: [laugh] I don't quite understand...
P: When does it become a homosexual attraction?
A: Huh?
P: When does it become a homosexual attraction?
A: Well, we're both of the same sex, aren't we?
P: Yeah.
A: Doesn't that sort of make it homosexual?
P: Well, when you, when I say homosexual, I think just in terms of the physical act, and I read somewhere that sex is behind every friendship. You know, whether it's with a guy or a girl, you know. If there wasn't any sexual a-attraction at all, you really couldn't have a friendship with anybody.
A: Well, that may be. But at present, it sounds a good deal as if you're calling on that to allay your fears.

The therapist fails to recognize that for the patient the word "homosexual" means a physical act and brushes this aside by his interpretation of the defense.

P: Yeah. Right. Well, I'm afraid of it and I freely admit that, you know.

A: You know, maybe we could put that together with your not coming yesterday. Maybe you felt that the kinds of interpretations I was making on Monday were the same thing and you couldn't come yesterday 'cause you were scared of this faggot here — who was gonna make a pass at you.

P: It's almost as if I don't want you to get the idea that I'm trying to pursue you and at the same time, I can almost get an indication of whether you're trying to pursue me or not, you know. Like, if I came in here and you were pissed off, you know, I'd be really afraid, you know, I'd say: "Fuck me, man, you know, this guy's really after my ass or something."

The progressive clarification of the meaning of the patient's skipping the appointment is impressive. So, too, is the fact that the initiative is primarily coming from the patient, although the analyst's pursuit of what in reality might make the patient's conjecture plausible certainly helps the patient continue.

At the same time, it is possible that the patient and the therapist are overlooking an enactment of the patient's homosexual wish through his subtle compliance with the therapist's expectations during the hour. For example, the very insight that the interaction with the man on the boat had transference implications may have been experienced as submission to the analyst in the here-and-now since it is the sort of connection the patient knows the analyst would like to hear him make.

A: Oh, you mean, if I were pissed off. . .

P: Yeah.

A: About your not having come. . .

P: But as long as, you know, nothing changed and you just said, "Well, that's the way it goes," you know.

A: That means I don't need you so desperately. I'm not after your ass.

P: Right.

A: I see. So another slight wrinkle that we can add to your not coming yesterday was that you thought Monday I might be too strongly attracted to you...

P: Well, Monday seemed to go real well and I really wondered why, you know.

A: That's what you couldn't stand, isn't it?

P: And— yeah.

A: And then...

P: Oh, I thought: "Jesus, you know, why did I come in here so eagerly or why did I open up so well?" And maybe subconsciously, I thought, you know—all these maybes and shit thrown in, but I'm—[sigh]. That I may have reacted in a way—"Well, you're really pushin' today, you know, or you're really in tune with what's happenin' or you're the one that wants to get back in with both feet."

A: Me?

P: Yeah. You've been away for a whole week, you know, and you gotta get back and secure me, you know.

A: Oh yes. I was too eager to recapture your love.

P: Yeah.

A very nice example of the reality anchorage of the transference. The therapist's "Me?" indicates that although he did not see it, he is receptive to the patient's idea. Still, the way the patient experiences the analyst's activity has not been made explicit. The interventions in the above segment might well be experienced by the patient as having an intense, driven quality, to which he may feel he is submitting.

A: So you stayed away a day partly to test to see whether it's true that I'm out to get you, and you were gonna judge that by how upset I got about your not having been here.

P: Yeah. But in any case, I [sigh] [pause], I don't know. I just had the image of, uh—like a guy and a broad, you know, and one does, you know, like, goes out with somebody else or something, you know, and the other partner gets pissed and says, "Well, fuck you, I'll go out with somebody else too."

A: Oh, that's it now. You had a date with another fellow yesterday instead of coming here—that's how you expect me
to respond: "So you like his company more than mine,
huh? OK." Hmm?

P: [pause] I don't know. All of a sudden, I got tremendously
uneasy and afraid, you know, when you [laugh] said, "Oh,
you had a date with another fellow, huh?"

A: [laugh] I was just translating what you said.

The therapist is forgetting that he was away and had cancelled
several appointments before the patient's failed appointment, so
that it could be that the patient identifies himself with the jealous lover who retaliates. This might explain why the patient is
stunned when he hears the analyst assume the jealous lover's
voice. In any case, a careful inquiry into what made the patient
uneasy would have been useful here.

P: I know, but that's just—I know, but that's just. . .

A: But you didn't like to hear the words coming out of somebody else's mouth, huh?

This remark is probably off-target. The patient may have become uneasy because he momentarily had the impression that
the therapist's words were intended quite literally as a confes-
sion of his attitude.

P: No. No. [pause] That's one of the things that produces a
lot of silences in me, you know. I wonder if you're gonna,
right away, make some kind of sexual overtone interpretation type of thing, you know, and. . .

A: No. I don't quite get that. What— you mean, at a point at
which you. . .

P: I try to avoid this whole line of discussion. [laugh] Well, I
do, you know.

A: Oh, you mean—I see, you mean the silences come at a
time when you had something in mind that you thought I
might have made a sexual interpretation about.

P: Yeah. Right.

A: Homosexual, that is.

The patient has made clear that he attaches a very special meaning to this word and that he doesn't want it used otherwise. But the analyst insists on it.

P: Right. Like, I try to watch what I say 'cause in the past, you know, you've jumped on, to me, perfectly innocent words, you know, and twisted them around and everything else, you know, and I've reacted finally to that. You know, now I don't know whether they're innocent or not but [sigh] it just seems to me that you're overzealous to prove that there's a sexual thing, you know, somewhere.
A: Mmm-hmm. And your interpretation of that overzealousness is a homosexual interest on my part.

It would have been better to delineate just what the patient finds "overzealous." The interpretation that the patient wants to make the therapist jealous by having a "date" with another man might well be what the patient finds "overzealous."
    At the same time, this is a nice example of an interpretation that picks up a repercussion on the transference of an earlier interpretation of the transference. The interpretation of homosexuality is taken as a homosexual approach. But it is not just the content which is in question. It is the mode—what the patient experiences as "overzealousness."

P: Evidently, yeah. You know, I don't think about it or feel about it, but, you know, I know I do run and I really don't know why and that would be a helluva good reason. [pause] I don't know. [pause] I'm always uptight about other people thinking I'm a faggot because—. I know that they know that I don't go out with women, and I don't, you know, and I can't just say: "Oh, Jesus, I'm afraid, man, you know. I'm chicken shit." What can you say?
A: Sounds a little like you think you're never gonna be able to still your doubts about that until you can actually make it with a woman.

A departure from the transference. It would have been better

for the analyst to stick with the "overzealousness." He may be
joining the patient in shying away from an idea that makes both
participants uncomfortable.

P: Yeah. Right. That's the way I feel anyway. That'd be just
     one more goddam added burden, though—if the situation
     ever arose, let's say. Oh, Jesus, you know, I gotta finally
     prove to myself, you know, this thing here and—so...
A: Mmm. That helps a little explain why the situation seems
     so alarming and challenging and full of terrible potential
     for you, because if you should not be able to make it, you
     would feel—"Oh, my God, I am homosexual." [pause]
     You got an awful lot riding on that card.

The analyst recognizes the anxiety but not in the transference.

P: Yeah. I know. That's no shit. [pause] And I don't know
     why I do things like that, you know—put all my eggs in
     one basket. I've done that, in the past, with other things,
     you know, like, uh, my personal appearance. All the eggs
     are in one basket—you know, when I lose weight, I will
     improve my personal appearance. I'll go out and buy some
     new clothes and I'll take care of myself and all this other
     shit—that's all my eggs in one basket there. School, I put
     all my eggs in one basket too. You know, I'm gonna get an
     "A" or I'm not gonna go—period. [laugh] It almost seems
     as if I have to make the test super-hard. [pause] You know,
     gotta be an immediate success or [sigh] doomed to failure
     forever. I don't know. [pause] All different words for mak-
     ing a mountain out of a molehill. [pause] I don't know.
     Why is my perspective all screwed up? [sigh] That's the
     other side of the coin about—"Oh, I get hurt too easily,"
     you know. Seems like everything is out of proportion.
     [pause] Be nice if I could set everything up on a scale of
     one to ten and say—well, for this, I'll always react at the
     three level, and for this, I'll always react at the five level,
     and for this, I'll always react at the two level, you know. It
     seems like I'm either zero or ten all the time. And I've been
     aware of this for awhile now and I don't know why I need

to preserve it so, you know. I talk about it but — shit — it's
still the same. I hang onto it.

A: To what?

P: These extremes. To me, I consider them extremes.

A: You slipped away from concrete talking about what it,
what you're afraid of in your relationship with me and how
it would feel to challenge yourself, etc., with a woman and
so on — I think you slipped away from that to a relatively
abstract discussion of the nature of extremes.

True, but there may be some allusion to the transference in the
content nonetheless. For example, there may be a hidden continuing criticism of the analyst's going to extremes — of his overzealousness.

P: Yeah. Well, if you could answer that abstract, you know,
maybe you might give me some heart in the concrete. I
don't know.

A: [pause] Obviously, it's my impression — belief — that these
questions don't get answered in the abstract.

The patient returns criticism for criticism, but the analyst defends himself rather than examining the interaction.

P: Yeah. I know. [pause] And then it's just more talk. [laugh]

A: I think so. [pause] I do notice, for example — this is not to
take you away from talking about us — that — so you, you
went out on, you went with him on a boat and you haven't
said a word about what it was like.

P: Oh, yeah.

A: An early word that the weather was nice or something. I
don't know if you were on a sailboat or a stink pot or what.

Here the analyst decidedly takes the discussion away from the
relationship. Although it is true that we have learned very little
about what actually happened on the trip and that if we did we
might gain further clues to the transference, at the same time
the exploration of the transference seems to be proceeding well

without this information. The therapist, however, has several times interrupted that exploration.

P: [laugh] No. It was a motor boat. Went all the way to Lake Z. It was kinda like weird because there wasn't too many other...

A: You went to Lake Z? From where?

P: Uh, D [place]. I don't know, it's about five, six miles.

A: I don't know the topography. Is there a river?

P: It's the K—the drainage canal for the city, you know, and it's all shitty and then you get by the lakes—you know, almost to Lake Z there, and they have a big docking area, and it's all polluted and shit, you know, and there's dust and everything else in the air, but, uh...

A: Of course, what I'm more interested in is what you referred to as a charged atmosphere.

P: Oh. [pause] I don't know. It's almost as if I, I had a good time, you know. But it wasn't, you know— I didn't allow myself to get really excited and everything, you know, and I should have, because I never get on a boat—or very rarely—and I went through a lock for the second time in my life, you know, but I kept reminding myself saying: "Well, now be cool and stay casual and don't come across like a, like a little kid or whatever."

A: For fear—that he would think you're queer.

P: Well. Yeah. Or at least—at the very least—an asshole, you know.

A: Oh. Only assholes get excited.

P: Yeah. Assholes or queers. [laugh] You know, you're just supposed to take it and say: "Hey, yeah, that was all right, you know. What are we gonna do tomorrow? Same old shit?"

A: Keep it cool.

The patient speaks of being cool and not acting like a little kid. The analyst at once returns to the theme of homosexuality. The patient may experience this as overzealousness—as not "cool"— and hence as homosexual in itself. Yet the patient does take up the word "queer." The analyst then returns to "cool," more in line with where the patient is.

P: Yeah. Right. [pause] More like overreact—you know, you're not supposed to overreact—that's a cardinal sin. And usually when I do, I get clumsy anyway, you know—I was very uptight about that, you know. I didn't ask him to drive the boat once, you know, except to park it, you know, coming back—put it up on a trailer—but, uh, you know, I didn't want to fuck up. There's a lot of logs in the canal and you hit one, you punch a hole in the boat. But I had a good time anyway. It was fast. Did about 55—on the water. I don't know. Like, I can remember when I was a little kid, you know, I'd get excited about something, you know, and I'd immediately fuck it up. As a matter of fact, the last time I was on a boat, I got to drive it, you know, and pull some skiers, and I threw it into reverse with the bridle and the tow rope on the back end of it and cut the bridle, you know. [laugh] And if you haven't got a spare bridle, you don't ski any more that day. Plus you screw up the motor and everything else.

A: [pause] Sounds also like you feel I lost my cool Monday. Got too excited about being back with you and the fun that we had—you said I jumped in with both feet.

The analyst returns to the transference and makes another useful connection to the patient's experience of the situation. However, he pulls the rug out from under the patient by returning to the transference without any transition and without acknowledging the patient's manifest concerns. Also, the interpretation itself might have been better had it mentioned the possibility that the patient specifically intended to warn the therapist of the dangers of getting too excited.

P: [sigh] Yeah. But the way you jumped in was kind of a negative way, you know. You didn't sit here and probe everything. You pretty much let me talk.

A: Well, how then is that jumping in with both feet?

P: I almost got the feeling that I was kind of wandering a little bit, you know, but you weren't too concerned about it, you know. You wanted to make sure that you were back and everything was OK before you started pumping again, you know—"Well, let's talk about this today and. . ."—"Well, let's be concerned with this and let's observe that."

The manner in which the therapist's behavior is translated into a sexual idiom is striking.

A: Oh, I see. The very fact that I didn't probe means to you that I wanted to make love first to be sure that everything is OK.
P: Yeah. You know. . .
A: That's jumping in with both feet. I was too friendly.

An interesting example of how even apparently opposite behaviors on the analyst's part lend themselves to the same experience of the relationship on the patient's part. But the therapist does seem to be too active. Why didn't he let the patient finish his thought?

P: Yeah. Right. You know. . .
A: So you ran away. . .
P: It leads to distrust in me.
A: What?
P: It leads to distrust in me, you know.
A: It leads to your conviction that, as you put it, I'm after your ass. [laugh] So you stayed away Tuesday.
P: Yeah. [pause] Well, I didn't want to be misled into anything, you know—so. Or tricked, you know. You know, here I was thinking, you know: Oh, geez, you know, it's been a week and I really stored all up—stored this stuff all up—and then I'm just gonna overpower you, you know, and say what I want to say, and fuck you, man, I deserve it, you know, and gonna say—. Ah, it's a devious plot all along, you know—that's what you had in mind. [laugh] And then you're gonna nail me to the wall tomorrow. Say —"Well, it's all fine and good, you know, and you made your feeble effort, you know, and now we'll go back to my way of doing things."

Here the patient may be alluding implicitly to what just happened when, after his animated presentation of his actions on the boat (p. 109), the analyst dismissed the manifest content of these associations with a rather cavalier transference interpretation.

A: [laugh] That's another one of those you're never gonna let me forget.
P: Nope. Nope. I don't like feeling feeble at all. [pause] And I kinda knew you'd react that way as soon as I said "feeble." But. . . [sigh]

These somewhat unclear remarks apparently refer to the preceding session. Evidently the analyst used the phrase "feeble effort" about the patient and hurt his feelings. The patient experiences the analyst as plotting and condescending. Again, this suggests that the therapist's activity is the aspect of the interaction that the patient plausibly interprets as betraying the therapist's wish for homosexual dominance. It's a question of who will overpower whom in the verbal exchange. If the therapist indeed used the expression "feeble effort," the patient may have experienced this as the therapist's claiming a homosexual conquest over him.

A: You read me like a book.
P: Now I detect a note of sarcasm.
A: [laugh] Not [patient laughs] — not exclusively. But I think you probably were right that you knew that that would, that would elicit that kind of a response.
P: Yeah. I almost got the impression that if I were able to read you like a book, you'd think that was bad, you know. I think you take some pride in the fact that you're inscrutable or whatever — mysterious.

The patient probably experiences this banter as evidence that the therapist feels he has to be on top. He is notably free, however, to express his assessment of the analyst's behavior — testifying perhaps to the atmosphere of openness that the analyst has succeeded in creating.

A: I thought that was your conviction that that's what a

proper analyst is. You say. . .

P: Yeah.

A: You say that I come down the hall with my entourage; I take great pains to show them that I reveal to you nothing. [pause] So you like a lot of advance notice about a. . .

P: [laugh] Goin' away mister.

A: Well, I told you I'd be gone and. . .

P: Yeah. Sure.

A: The dates—I just fixed the dates so, uh. . .

P: Well, OK.

The analyst reacts somewhat defensively to the charge that he takes pride in being inscrutable. Then he attacks the patient by subtly suggesting that his need for advance notice of a separation is a weakness. The patient confessed earlier in the hour that separation led to the uncomfortable realization that he cares about the therapist.

A: Let's see, the last day will be Monday, um—the last day in April. Then I'm not quite sure whether we will resume on Tuesday or Wednesday. If you would be able to make an appointment late in the afternoon, I might be able to resume Tuesday.

P: Of what?

A: Oh, that's right. I didn't say of what. Well, it's a week later. The, uh—the 8th.

P: May 8th?

A: Yeah. We meet April 30th, Monday, and then not again until either. . .

P: This is the big convention. Where was it last year—Dallas?

A: Right. You mean you know this is the time of the year for the convention?

P: Yeah.

A: So there's no point in concealing that. This year it's in Honolulu.

P: Oh, wow. It must be nice. Kind of one step above Dallas. The reason I'm aware of it is because in the group I was in last year, one of the doctors went to the convention and one of the guys in the group had her traced, you know. It was really weird, boy, you know. He was really involved, you know.

A: You mean, he wanted to be sure she was at work and not having fun.

The possible allusion to the patient's involvement is more to the point.

P: Yeah. [analyst laughs] Well, he had detectives on her for a long time, you know.
A: Detectives?
P: Yeah. He was really off the wall — still is, you know. I don't go to see them much anymore.
A: That have something to do with you. . .
P: That has something to do with my fear of getting involved, you know. I say: "Hey, man, will I fuck myself up?"
A: You mean, it can get, become so extreme. . .
P: Yeah. You go off the deep end.
A: You really go off the deep end, right.

The patient makes the interpretation himself and the analyst accepts it.

A: Have I done something wrong now in admitting to you. . .

Why is he prejudicing the patient's experience? Done wrong? Admit? The likelihood is that he feels he has violated one of the taboos of his training; it is the analytic community to which he is speaking.

P: Oh, no, you know. But I don't think I would pursue the matter if I asked and you didn't tell me.
A: Yes. Well, we were talking about, uh, resuming, and as I say, it would be either, uh, late Tuesday, or if not, then Wednesday.
P: Yeah. Well, I can probably make it late Tuesday. That's been my habitual day off. Seeing as we're going through — I don't know — I'll have to let you know for sure before you leave.

A: OK.

P: But I'm sure we can work it out—all right. 'Cause I got T [special event] starting next week. Everything'll be up for grabs. I don't think that I'm gonna miss anything down here, you know, but I don't know what to expect at work. Everything might change.

A: I don't understand. You don't think you're gonna miss what?

P: I don't think I'll miss anything down here, you know, but with T, you know, you're asshole over elbow and everything else and. . .

A: Oh, I'm sorry. You mean, there's T, but you think you'll be here anyhow.

P: Yeah.

A: I see. When is that week?

P: Uh, next week. But, you know, I have the people at work locked in that, you know, my hour is sacrosanct.

A: Unless you have to take a boat ride.

The analyst is responding to the patient's sarcasm with some of his own. The remark certainly seems pertinent, although it is important to be sensitive to the way the patient may take such needling.

P: Yeah. Right. But they don't know that.

A: [laugh] I know.

P: I got my priorities. Work is last, right about now. And you might be second to last. So—. [slight pause] And I'm somewhere in the middle. I'm not first by any means but, uh, I gotta have a higher priority than you.

A: To yourself, you mean?

P: Yeah. [laugh] Yeah. That's right. [pause]

A: Time is up.

P: So long.

A: Bye.

Is the patient making a joke too? Is the banter a covert homosexual interaction?

Additional Comments

Despite the lapses we have noted, we rate this hour high. Our notes on the session were made with the knowledge that the patient would soon interrupt the analysis, allegedly for a reality reason. We may therefore have been inclined to overemphasize the therapist's activity as having unbearable homosexual implications for the patient.

6

PATIENT F: SESSION 147

INTRODUCTION

This session illustrates how the analyst's reluctance to take the patient's experience of the relationship seriously, apparently because he dislikes its implications for him, interferes with the examination of that experience. At the same time, the very fact that the analyst is attempting to follow our principle of finding the plausible basis for the patient's experience of the relationship makes his failure to follow the principle through and the consequences of that failure especially clear and vivid.

The reader may feel that the primary fault in the analyst's technique is his excessive activity. While we agree that his activity is more than optimal, we wish to emphasize that it is not his activity per se that is the main problem but rather the fact that this activity specifically shuts off an elaboration of the patient's perceptions of the therapist. In other words, it is not simply the *amount* of activity that is the problem. An equivalent quantity of activity appropriately directed would not necessarily be faulty technique. We should, however, add that such activity may well have implications for the patient's experience which are not explored. This may be true even if the activity consists of interventions that seem to accurately explicate what the patient is implying.

In the session presented here, the patient may well experience the analyst's activity in a number of ways, ranging from impatience with her (the patient) to a solicitous effort to make it easier for her. The analyst should explore how the patient experiences his active behavior, just as he should explore the patient's experience of any aspect of his behavior, including silence. Again, we are voicing our disagreement with the belief that silence is good and that its effects do not require examination while activity is automatically suspect.

THE ANNOTATED SESSION

A: Hello.
P: Hi. I brought your check, but I, I haven't forgotten it. But I forgot to bring it. Mmm—I have forgotten it. I just remembered. [pause]
A: Do you feel it has to be brought in the very next time after you get the bill?
P: Well, yeah, I usually do. Yeah. I usually like to pay bills as soon as I get them. Right now, we have, uh—probably for the first time—so many bills [laugh] that, that, uh, I'm not paying them. I'm just letting them sit there. The big one being the 600 dollars for my teeth. I'll just have to pay part, but, uh—but yeah, I, I like to get them paid. That's the bills basically—the rent and our other bills. That's not—I mean, that's not the charge— we don't have charge accounts. But, but yes, I guess, I, I—. [pause] My dad is with me. [pause] I, I haven't sat down and talked to him yet but. . .
A: You have not? When did he come in?
P: Yesterday afternoon.
A: And how long is he staying?

Some might regard these as "social" questions which are not conducive to an "analytic" atmosphere. From our point of view, the only consideration that is of technical importance is whether the analyst pays attention to the effects of such an exchange on the patient's experience of the interaction.

P: Until Thursday afternoon. And today, I went to work, and tomorrow, I don't have to and— well, last night, we went to W [place] for supper. And I guess it's OK. I was real worried this morning that no one was gonna stay home with him and R [husband] told me that, uh, I do that with

everybody who comes to visit so—. But then Daddy came
down to the store. He'd walked around campus. It stopped
raining which was nice. It's true, he's capable— anyway he
came to see us, he didn't come to see N [city]. So it'd be
kinda bad if he didn't spend any time with us. [pause] I'm
worried but I can't put my finger on it. I'm worried about
my dad being here. For instance, I'm worried about, I'm
worried about, I guess, all our conversations last week but
I can't quite figure out why, why it's worrisome. [short
pause] I don't know, maybe the week got off to a bad start
because I, you know, I thought you were gonna be here
Monday. [laugh] I— that just— I, I just had a feeling that
things aren't right. You know, things aren't going quite the
way they should be going. [pause] I'm trying to remember
something I thought [laugh] you said. I didn't think much
this weekend, I spent eight and a half hours at the co-op
collecting signatures. Just needed to go home, have a glass
of wine, fall asleep for 12 and a half hours. I don't know
how— what it— I don't think— I mean, it was OK but it
just, it's just gonna take so much out of me, I don't know
how often I'll be able to do it. But—. [pause] You know, I
have the sense that I spent all— I talked a lot last week and
spent a lot of time— trying to, uh—. Well, what's wrong
with that? But to try and clarify my position, you know,
and to sort of argue my position in a way, but I'm— I—
I— all I can think of now is the name business, you know.
That. . . [pause]

A: Have you any idea what is motivating you to read a book
    like that?
P: To, to read what? The case book?
A: The case book. Mmm-hmm.

This could be explained to the reader, but in the interest of seeing whether the session can stand alone and be understood, we
have chosen not to do so.

P: I stopped reading it. I haven't read any more but, uh [sigh],
    probably a lot of things. One is that it— I, I find— well, I
    wouldn't be surprised if part of it was that— I wouldn't be

surprised if part of it was— maybe I'm [?] thinking that
this is what you're fishing for. But that's, uh—. I can't figure that out right off. Uh—. Thinking that you will write a
book that is similar, in a way. Although, I have no way of
knowing that and there's certainly other possibilities. I was
also thinking about how psychotherapists think about what
they're doing. It was interesting. I also— I got a pleasure
out of reading them—case studies—I've done— that's happened for a long time. I read them, in a certain sense— I
read them like I read fiction or biographies or I read, you
know, I read them, you know, I read—they, you know,
give me pleasure. I like to read them. [laugh] I like to read
them better than other stuff. And, of course, the H
[psychiatrist] books have been there a long time and I
haven't— I've been tempted to read them but that would
be work, you know, unless I can just read, you know, like
[?], and I, you know, I mean, there's always a risk that I, I
read myself into a lot of things. I either— I say, "Oh, that's
what's wrong with me," so, I don't know, but that didn't
happen with this book—. I don't think.

A: Except for the name thing.
P: Well, I brought it up because I thought I was—you know
     —the difference, you know.
A: Oh, yes. That's right.
P: I mean, I didn't bring it up because I said, "Hey, you don't
     call me, you don't call me by my first name either." I brought
     it up; I said, well, you know, I was reading this case study.
     And what I was bringing up which is significant—I sort of
     wondered why you didn't point it out since you're always
     pointing things out—which is that this guy was trying out
     these new forms of— this new—not form— one, you
     know, new technique or whatever—interpretation he
     makes—he admitted that he made mistakes and it was in-
     teresting to see, you know, and also nice that he talked
     about the mistakes he made. And at the same time, that he
     kept this woman, that it may have well kept this woman in
     analysis significantly longer than if he hadn't, you know. I
     don't, I don't know if I was waiting for you or not to say:
     "Are you telling me that you think I'm, you're going to be

in analysis longer because I'm trying out something new?"
And [laugh] you didn't say it, but I thought it afterwards,
and I think that probably was what was significant from
reading that chapter and not the thing about the names at
all. And it's true that the names became significant, but I
don't think I really thought twice about it.

The patient has possibly become accustomed to the analyst's
pointing out allusions to the transference. She proposes such an
interpretation herself.

A: Well, I looked at the case again, by the way, and, uh, he
thinks as I, as I got it. . .
P: Mmm-hmm.
A: That maybe the analysis took longer because — not because
he was trying out something new — but because he was
stuck in the old. That is. . .

The remark is decidedly self-revelatory. He shows that he had
already read the case, and has now read it again, presumably in
response to her having referred to it.

P: OK. Well, right.
A: What?
P: All right. That's OK. I'll buy that.
A: That's right. Yes.
P: That's fine.
A: But I would like to draw your attention to something you
said when I first asked you the question. I imagine you
know what that is.
P: That I, that I may be saying what you're fishing for.

Two things are noteworthy. The analyst returns to her immediate
response (p. 120, line 2) to his question, which implied a meaning
the question had for her in her experience of the interaction. Furthermore, instead of saying what her response was, he gives her a
chance to do so, thus establishing that she, too, had registered it.
But might this also be experienced as a kind of "fishing"?

A: Right.

P: Mmm-hmm.

A: You don't take the question as a question. You think I have a preconception and I'm not asking to find out what the reason might be that you're reading the book in a sort of a —quote—innocent way, but I'm fishing for something and I think that, uh, it's kind of characteristic of how you see this relationship. That if I ask a question, it's, uh—. A kind of a, uh, trick, possibly. Yes?

Now, instead of finding out what the patient meant by "fishing" and exploring her ideas about his motivation, the analyst implies that the patient is characteristically, without sound reasons, suspicious of his intentions. By quickly blaming the patient, the analyst cuts off a thorough investigation of the patient's perceptions of him.

P: Well, we've talked about that. Yes.

A: We have. I know. But that. . .

P: Not to say that's not true, but yes. . .

The analyst seems to have succeeded in disarming the patient. It would have been better if he had helped her to develop and elaborate her point.

A: You are not saying it's not true, and it remains, apparently, as some kind of a constant silent background to our interaction—how you see my, how I relate to you.

P: Mmm-hmm.

A: There's a suspiciousness there.

P: Mmm-hmm. See, that was the nice thing about reading those two case studies that I did that, at least, well, there was some, there were some preconceptions, but there was a lot less of it than I thought.

A: Than you thought what?

P: Than I thought psychoanal—, analysts would have.

A: As characteristic of analysts.

P: That's right.

A: Nevertheless, you attributed it to me.

P: Well, that's right. But I mean, but I mean, you read the book, you know.

A: But, uh —. Well, what do you mean?

P: I just — in saying that "yes, that's true" — I do attribute it to you and, and yet — and, and I — and just to further that same point, I was surprised in reading this book that, in fact, my assumptions weren't borne out in this text I was reading so, uh —. I'm just saying, you know, that that was another place where I recognized it, where I . . .

A: You seem to be making something of a distinction between whether your suspiciousness is based on some general concept of what analysts are like or whether it has to do with how you feel about me. That — do you understand the distinction I'm making? Almost as if — if you are suspicious of me in the aspect that we've been talking about, it would be because that's what analysts are like, not because it's me.

P: [pause] And you mean 'cause that's a distinction that can't be made?

A: The distinction can be made, but I am suggesting, more implicitly than explicitly, that, uh — I suspected that your suspiciousness of me won't be particularly influenced by what you read about what analysts do.

P: Mmm-hmm.

A: Because some analysts can be suspicious and others not. In other words, I think it has to do with us, not with ideas about analysis. That might be a convenient way of — as a matter of fact — of making, making it more impersonal.

P: Mmm-hmm. To say . . .

A: To say it has to do with ideas about analysis, not about me.

The analyst is clearly determined to keep the immediate interaction sharply in focus. He seems to have forgotten, however, that he has, himself, discouraged the patient from pursuing specific ideas about him by referring to her characteristic tendency to interpret his "questions" as "tricks" (p. 127, lines 2–7), in effect disparaging her understanding of his behavior.

P: Right. Yeah. That's true. So I —. I don't think I read it primarily to find out about you but —. I don't think, I don't think — I'm sorry — I don't think that's what you are saying. I meant — I wanted to say that.

A: What? If there was any fishing, it was only in terms of my wondering whether your reading the book has anything to do with the analysis, and it could be any number of things.

The analyst seems defensive about the "fishing," enough so that he apparently overlooks her remark about not having read the case to find out about him and the apologizing—all clearly important in the interaction. Moreover, he seems to imply that the sense in which he may have been fishing is rather minor or trivial. But, in fact, it may well be exactly this sense the patient has in mind, namely, that he wants her to make the connection to the analysis, and for her this may not be a trivial demand at all.

P: It, it probably does, you know.

A: Well, I think it might be. . .

P: My being in analysis probably has something to do with my reading these kinds of books too, you know, so—. I haven't read a whole lot but I mean, there's an interest there that, that is something— there is an interest there, I mean, you know, for like—. And actually, probably the main reason I'm here is because I was in therapy before, but, but then, of course, that shaped my interest too, I mean, so, I mean, you know, it's— it, uh. . .

A: I meant something specific; to give an example of what did occur to me might be your reasons.

P: Mmm-hmm.

A: Though—. Can we distinguish between my thinking something might be a reason and not fishing for that reason? Is that, that. . .

P: Maybe. I'll try. [laugh]

A: [laugh] I mean, it occurred to me that if I would tell you I had an idea about what might be the reason, that you would think you could consider that justification of your view that I was fishing for that, and I'm asking if. . .

P: Mmm. No. OK.

A: I think there's a distinction and asking if you can. . .

P: Yeah. I think there's a distinction.

Again, the analyst seems quite defensive about the "fishing."

What needs to be explored is the patient's own sense that she might be merely complying with what she imagines his expectations are. Among other things, what does she think would happen if she did not comply? What does she imagine would be his inner reaction, as well as his outward response? After all, it appears she may have cause for concern since she has stirred up such a barrage of defensive counterarguments just by using the word "fishing."

A: You can. OK. That perhaps, you feel—and I do remember that we have talked about this before...

P: Mmm-hmm.

A: That you'd like to know more about this process...

P: Mmm-hmm.

A: And I'm not engaging in talking with you about the process. Maybe, therefore, you're turning to the book to try to get something that you're not getting from me that you might like to get.

P: That's possible. Because I—yeah—because I— when it goes— like today, when I feel it's not going well, you know, I don't know—. It hasn't really, it hasn't really upset me too much that I haven't been able to say why I think it goes well. But I'm curious, you know, and I always think— or if I'm talking to R or somebody, I'll say, "Well, I hope before I'm finished, I'll know"—you know. I'll have some hint of why, why it helps. Why it, you know—. And now, most of the time, you know—like, I have these senses now, sort of like that—you know—when people ask me, "Well, how is therapy?" I say, "Well, it's, it's going very well," you know.

A: Oh, so, perhaps, when you said today...

P: And then I think—but why, you know, why? Why is that?

A: You had—. You don't know why.

P: And today I don't know why either, you know.

A: And today, you don't know why it's not going well.

P: No.

A: Or why you have that sense, at any rate...

P: No. And I really do.

A: And perhaps, you were hoping that I would try to supply an answer.

P: Well, I hoped that maybe we could try to figure it out. Ex-
     cept that I don't have too much to go on, except that I—.
     And I wish I could—. And—well, what. . . [pause]
A: Something happened, uh, at the end of the last session. . .

The patient's remark immediately above about "figuring it out"
suggests she rejects the implication that she is expecting the analyst to feed her an answer. Perhaps he fails to take this up because he has been waiting to introduce what happened at the
end of the previous session.

P: [pause] I can't remember.
A: You can't remember. Mmm-hmm. [patient laughs] What
     I had in mind—that you said something to me and didn't
     get a reply.
P: I said, "Have a nice weekend."
A: So you did. [patient laughs]

Again, the analyst alludes to something by a hint and the patient supplies what he had in mind.

A: Were you aware of any response to that or—. That was
     unusual.
P: No. That was the first time.
A: Uh, what was that about? By which I mean, why then
     and. . .
P: And never before.
A: And did you have any reaction to no reply and— obvious-
     ly, I'm bringing that up now to, uh, ask whether that might
     play some role in this sense of dis-ease.

Perhaps this explanation is offered because of some uneasiness
on the analyst's part about having brought up the issue himself.

P: [pause] I think the dis-ease is, uh— but I guess not. Be-
     cause dis-ease, dis-ease—the part of, part of it is that—.
     But see, now I can't remember why and what—why I got
     this feeling. Just afraid that I was, that I was gonna be such
     a good talker and that I, that you weren't going to be able

to help me, you know, that I was gonna, uh— I was gonna shut you up, I guess.

A: I'm sorry. I don't hear a bridge. Uh, how did you get to that?

Since he does not follow what she is saying at a manifest level, he asks for clarification.

P: I had said— 'cause I don't—well, because I don't have any association with—"have a good weekend." But, uh...

A: When were you afraid you'd be such a good talker, you'd shut me up?

P: This weekend. [pause] But why I said, "Have a good weekend," I don't know, you know.

A: I'm sorry. I'm really not following you. This weekend you had the thought—. Yes...

P: I just had the feeling that some— that it didn't go well last week. That it was not a good week, you know. That—and I don't know, I don't know why that is really—but the feeling was that, that I just talked and talked and talked, you know, and maybe I didn't even do that, you know, but that...

A: You mean, this was a tentative explanation you gave yourself for why you had the feeling that it wasn't a good week and the, and the tentative explanation was that you talked and talked and talked...

P: That's right and that you were...

A: ...and maybe shut me up.

P: 'Cause you just weren't, you're just not— that it was...

A: That I wasn't what?

P: That you, you—. Oh, I can't remember. Some—. I have these conversations with you in my head, you know, I should tape-record them.

A: Did you get tearful a little bit ago?

Rather than continuing with the verbal exchange, the analyst calls attention to evidence of an immediate emotional response.

P: Yes. A little bit.

A: What about?

P: Well, because I, I want to be able to tell you about this and I don't—I can't, I can't do it.

A: And the tearfulness is—what?

P: 'Cause it's very important and I— and, and I'm frustrated because I'm not— I— because it's—[slight pause] I don't know, it's very, it's more than worrisome, in fact. It was true that—. [pause] Why did I say, "Have a good weekend"? I don't know.

A: What?

P: Yes. I was very aware of saying it.

A: Uh. . .

P: I don't think I minded that you weren't saying anything back. Because I said it and sort of ran away. Uh. . .

A: Is that what you meant was important—that exchange? Or lack of exchange?

P: Mmmm.

A: I wasn't quite clear.

P: No. No. [pause]

A: No.

While her saying she ran away suggests an important meaning of the event, the analyst is more interested first in clearly understanding the manifest connections.

P: What's important is my being able to tell you why I was so worried that you wouldn't be able to help me. Uh—. But I started to answer your question. There was something, something that. . .

A: You mean, over the weekend, you had this idea—first of all, that it hadn't gone very well and then—do I understand correctly?—that connected with that is the idea that you talked and talked and talked and I wouldn't be able to help you because you had to shut me up. Is that it?

P: Yeah. That, that's as far as I've gotten—. And I sense that there's something more, and I even figured out something more, but I can't figure it out now, but [pause] I may have said it to feel less bad. [pause]

A: Oh, your. . .

P: Saying—I may have said. . .

A: Saying. . .

P: "Have a good weekend." Because. . .

A: Because you were trying to patch up something that you felt wasn't quite right.

Although she does seem to be implying something of this sort, his conclusion seems a bit hasty. He would probably do well to keep silent and just listen for awhile.

P: Uh-huh.

A: Oh.

P: I don't know. I mean. . .

A: You don't know.

P: I didn't — You know, I didn't. . .

A: But this is. . .

P: . . . contemplate it ahead of time. I didn't think. . .

A: Yes. I see.

P: . . . Well, today, I'm finally gonna say, "Have a good weekend," to Dr. M. I, you know — I didn't, so, I mean, it's just not. . .

A: The implication being that you had to make up to me for something, for shutting me up, perhaps? [pause] What you said about the talking a great deal was actually something rather different, as I remember.

Is it good technique for the analyst to say how he remembers it rather than to accept how the patient does — or at least explore further how she does? He seems to be repeatedly interrupting her, a habit which certainly is not good technique. Maybe her anxiety about shutting him up is associated with a wish to do so, combined with an impression that he likes to talk. One may wonder whether, in fact, he was quieter the previous week, thus giving her cause for some concern.

P: Mmm-hmm.

A: You, you, you were upset because you felt you had opened up a great deal, sort of. . .

P: That's right.

A: But hadn't tied things together neatly.

P: That's it.

A: So it wasn't so much that, uh...

P: That might be it too.

A: That might be what?

P: That might be it. I mean, that might be it, saying also that I, that I—I don't know—that it's scary to open up a lot of things and then be afraid that you're not gonna be able to put them all together.

A: But, perhaps, the feeling is then that I hadn't helped you because I had failed to put them together for you.

P: Well...[pause]

A: And then the idea that if you shut me up, uh— well, perhaps, uh, you're excusing me, as against blaming me, for failing to help by tying it together, and leaving you in that unraveled state.

P: Mmm-hmm. [pause] What was so confusing was that I wasn't even sure what I—. I don't like not knowing what I'm talking about. [laugh] [pause] And there's all these things—these little things, you know. I was, like, talking to you about being supportive and then—even though you said that, you know, there it is again, it's another question, right? [pause] Now that must mean something—here come the tears again. [laugh]

A: You said something about tears but I didn't quite get it.

P: I said that must mean something because when I said that, you know, and I just thought it, and all of a sudden, there were all these tears that were coming to the surface, but what I was thinking was I really wanted you to be supportive and then I felt, you know— all of a sudden, I got [?], I thought, "Oh, my God, I'm not supposed to want that," you know. I mean, that's just—I don't know—that's childish or something, uh, or that's not— I mean, that's just a temporary [?], I don't know. I don't care if it's temporary as long as it's not just temporary like for two hours, you know. [short pause] It might have something to do with—too, with [inaudible] and just being afraid that you wouldn't stick around. [pause] You know, that...

A: That I wouldn't stick around.

P: Mmm-hmm.

It is noteworthy that after the interpretation suggesting that she
is excusing him rather than blaming him, there is a flow of material which does reveal her distress about how he is behaving
and even leads to tears.

P: I guess I'm the one who might go to B [a foreign country].
A: I'm sorry. I can't...
P: I'm sorry. I said that I could—. Yes, that's, that's what I
      said— that's...
A: But then you said, "I guess I'm the one..."
P: I'm the one who's going to B, aren't I? It's not— you never
      said you were going anywhere. Except on vacation. Then
      you were late. Two minutes. And, of course, if I asked you
      not to think anything about my being late, I shouldn't wor-
      ry about your being late, right? And I was thinking about
      the name when I was sure I was right. [pause] And then
      you looked tired.
A: I looked tired?
P: Last week.
A: Yes. You said that. You know, it might be possible to sum-
      marize a lot of this by saying that your sense of things not
      being quite right is an expression of your uncertainty
      about my reliability.
P: Mmm-hmm.
A: Whether it be because I'm too tired to help you or will dis-
      appear or something, and, uh, I think it would be fair to
      say that if two minutes—not alone but with these other
      things—is enough to shake your sense of confidence in my
      reliability, we have some indication of how tenuous it is.
P: [short pause] Two minutes three days in a row.

She seems offended that he suggests such a small thing can
make her doubt his reliability. Actually, he has made the mistake again of too quickly calling into question her interpretation
of his behavior. As with the "fishing" episode, he starts off well,
as though he really wants to hear how she experiences him, but
then very quickly becomes defensive. In fact, in addition to the

lateness, she has mentioned several other things that may be affecting her idea of his reliability—his tiredness the previous week, for example, and her expectation that he would be in the office the previous Monday (p. 119; line 11) when apparently he was not.

A: It was two minutes three days in a row.

P: Mmm-hmm.

A: I was late three times?

P: Mmm-hmm. According to the clock in the hall. You weren't today.

A: Which clock—downstairs?

P: No. This one.

A: That one? Oh. . .

P: That— but I don't think that's a big thing. The first two days, as I said, I was relieved because I was late myself, so. . . [pause]

A: You don't think it's a big thing, but it sounds like you noticed it and added them up.

P: I noticed it. Yes.

A: Yes.

P: I guess that's because it's become pretty— you know, it's become an issue for me to get here on time so I do watch the clock pretty, pretty closely.

A: Well, when you said three days in a row. . .

P: Mmm-hmm.

A: . . .I thought you meant I was late two minutes.

P: You— that's right, but I mean, I'm watching the clock so I'm sensitive. . .

A: How did you know I was, if you were late? I'm not clear.

P: Because I got here and it was two minutes after. . .

A: Oh, you got here and I still. . .

P: And you hadn't opened your door.

A: Oh. [pause] You mentioned it only one time, is that right?

P: Mmm-hmm.

A: Why did you not tell me the other times?

Does her accusation beget a retaliatory accusation?

P: Because I didn't think it was worth mentioning.

A: Why not?

P: Because...

A: You noticed it.

P: That's right. But, I mean, I notice a lot of things and...

A: You attributed some important significance to it.

P: I don't think I did.

A: Oh, you don't think so. You think, maybe retrospectively, these things started to pile up, is that it?

This is rather more sympathetic to her point of view.

P: Yes.

A: I see. [pause] And what, then, did they mean—I'm losing interest in you, or what?

P: You didn't want to see me.

A: I don't want to see you because...

P: 'Cause it's going to be such a struggle.

A: Because?

P: 'Cause I, I just have, uh—I don't know—because I'm such a smart ass. 'Cause there's all these things that you don't, that I, you know—I mean, first it's the money and then it's the names and all these things, and I'm ambiguous and hard to deal with.

A: A smart ass. What was that?

P: I don't know. I didn't think—. I just thought that now. A smart ass is somebody who, I don't know, thinks she knows a lot.

A: So you're a difficult patient, right? Because you, you think you know a lot and you're gonna make a fuss about your name and...

P: Well, but I mean, you know, but there's things that...

A: Money...

P: ...you, you don't— that you haven't figured out, you know, or [inaudible] of it. That's not true, but are not— they're not, there're no hard and fast rules about it. And you said that, and, you know, and that's OK, and actually —the thing with the money—I really respected that, you know, and at the same time—then this thing with the name —I wasn't even anticipating that, you know. I mean, that was — . Although, you know, I brought it up, so. . . [sigh]

A: So if there are no hard and fast rules, uh, and if you're gonna make a fuss about these things, I'd rather have a more
compliant patient. Is that it?

P: Somebody who didn't touch all these sore, all these sore
points. That, that makes — that, that means you have to
work that much harder.

A: To think these through and try to resolve them.

P: Mmm-hmm. And I know I'm not supposed to be worried
about you, though.

A: [laugh] Said she — [patient laughs] thrusting home.

This could be further explained to the reader by reference to
earlier material. But even without such information we think it
clear that her remark was somewhat sarcastic.

P: I'm sorry. [laugh]

A: That's another thing I, I don't like about you — your tongue,
huh? Which occasionally you lose control over [both laugh]
and make one of these cracks.

P: I'm sorry.

A: What are you sorry about?

P: I don't know. Because I didn't — 'cause I'm spiteful. [laugh]

A: So that's another reason I'd rather exchange you for another patient.

P: Right.

A: You're a spiteful, sarcastic, smart ass, huh?

P: [inaudible]

A: What?

P: My poor fingers. [sigh] [pause] Huh. My father does that
too. I noticed that last night. He's always going "huh." So
I, I know where I picked that up from. So there are two of
us, there were two of us eating dinner going "huh" all the
time. [pause] [mumbling] I guess I want to know if that's
true. I want reassurance.

A: If what's true?

P: That it's not true — you, you — . That — because you think
I'm a terribly difficult person to be with and that you, you
know — . It's just dreary — not dreary, just uncomfortable —

and you don't have any idea of what's going on and you don't know how you're ever gonna [sigh] help me get anywhere. [pause]

A: So we...

P: And, of course, then there was the thing with the names, you know. I mean, I really, I really, you know, I really think— I can't remember everything I said, but I sounded pretty confident because I was pretty confident about how I felt about it, I think. I'm not sure, you know, I'm not sure.

A: Oh, I see. So that's another reason I don't like you. You have the temerity to pit your memory against mine.

P: That's right.

A: Is that what you meant?

P: Yes. And also that I—. I disagreed with you. You know, I mean, I don't think it's—I don't know how major it is, right? You know, but...

A: In any case, I don't like to be disagreed with. So I was right when I said you think I'd rather have a more compliant patient.

This outpouring of how she feels the therapist is displeased with her is impressive. It may be a continuing result of his interpretation which implied that is was all right to blame him (p. 130, lines 12–15). What is also noteworthy is that although she explicitly said she wanted reassurance, he gave it only in the form of accepting her fears. His laughter and direct labeling of her sarcasm may have also served as reassurance. The possibility of its being an erotically tinged exchange should probably also be kept in mind.

A: [pause] You know, I think it could be said that your idea that I would be unable to help you...

P: Mmm-hmm.

A: ...is a form of, uh, the thought that I may be feeling that I can't help you.

P: Mmm-hmm.

A: You hear the difference? You came in to say that you had the idea that I couldn't help you, as if that's your idea.

P: No. Yes. That's true. I think it's your idea. Is that what you mean?

A: But you're now saying it as if you think that's my idea, right?

P: Mmm-hmm. But, but they would go together, you know.

A: Well, yes.

P: I mean, I can't, I certainly couldn't say: "Oh, no. . .

A: You could feel that I. . .

P: . . . of course, you can help me." I mean, I can't, I can't do that.

A: But, you mean, the full thought could be your idea that I can't help you is based on your idea that I feel I can't help you. That's a different thought from just coming in to say. . .

P: Yeah.

A: 'Cause you could say that you think I can't help you when you feel that I think I can.

P: Mmm-hmm. Mmm-hmm.

A: Yes. So, in a way, you're saying that you feel I can't help you. I'm trying to find out if you were conscious of the idea that you think I feel I can't help you.

The interpretation is of identification in the transference, i.e., it suggests that she attributes to herself an idea she believes the therapist holds—namely, that he can't help her. His effort to find out whether she consciously thought he felt he couldn't help her is designed to validate the interpretation. Perhaps he has a research interest on the concept of identification in the transference and its validation. He seems to have belabored the point.

P: I was thinking— I, I don't— I think the real problem is, is—. You see, I am very curious about how this works, and this may be circuitous, but I really— there really are bridges here because, I mean—. And I am, you know—. I mean, I made some semi-sarcastic remarks about transference in that book but— I mean, what really just came to my head when you were saying that about my feeling that you thought that you couldn't help me, was thinking of telling you about the time that my fath—, I was telling my father about my, uh—oh, I don't know—my confusion about sex or something, and my mother, and he said, "F [patient's first name], I really can't help you." You know. And so that's what came to my mind, you know, and then—. But, you see, I don't know if I should just say that, you know— or is that, is that?—you know—. Then I— you know, part of, part of me says, "Well, Dr. M is going to say that that's taking away from talking about us," you know. And I sort of see that, you know, and partly think—. And then I—. And I, you know, I see that and sort of agree with that, you know.

There is rather clear evidence of how the patient has been affected both by this session and by her previous "schooling" in the course of the analysis. Her use of the word "bridge" and her semi-apology for seeming to be "circuitous" above go back to the analyst's use of the word "bridge" (p. 127) and his obvious interest in a logically coherent manifest account. Her saying she was semi-sarcastic is probably related to his explicitly focusing on her sarcasm. But in a wider context she clearly feels that associations which are not about the current interaction with the analyst may well be labeled "defensive" by him. This is one of the obvious dangers run by any technique that emphasizes one kind of material over another. Insofar as the patient is compliant, the emphasis will act as a suggestion directing associations. Nevertheless, this patient indicates some possible difference of opinion by saying she "sort of" agrees with the analyst, and the fact remains that she does verbalize her association. Actually, in this instance, the genetic material comes up in an optimal way from our point of view—that is, as an association to something that was explicated about the patient's experience of the immediate interaction.

A: That's the objection to saying it, you think. Yes.
P: And then...
A: Yes.
P: You know, but I, but I thought, you know, I think that in — I think that's part of you know. I think that it, [pause]
A: What's part of it?
P: I think I, you know, I mean, I think that I [laugh], I think

that, I think that's part of my—. But, you see, why does it
sound so superficial coming. . .? It really does— is that. . .?
Well, who knows why it does, but that to think of you as
unreliable, I think there were things that happened here
last week that made me think, worry about that. Not unreliable, but I mean sort of not— strong enough. You're reli-
able. You're here all the time but, uh— well, there's Monday. But then that was my mistake, because you really did
tell me that, I think, but. . .

It seems clear she is doubtful that the error was hers. He fails to
pick this up, however.

A: But you had the idea someway—I was. . .
P: But there, there, you know, but there've been other people
    that I wanted to rely on and I haven't been able to rely on,
    you know, and so, I mean, there's possibly some kind of
    connection there. I mean, but I don't want it—it can't be
    just—. So, yes, so I mean, I do think there's, you know— I
    mean, I just do. . .
A: What happened last week that made you think I might not
    be strong enough?

This is the optimal question at this point because it invites the
patient to speak openly about her perceptions of the analyst
(very probably a point of resistance).

P: I don't know. I really don't know. [pause]
A: But, in any case, let me summarize for a moment. I gather
    that this idea about your father that was, that was what
    made you use the word "transference," as if. . .

It probably would have been better to keep silent here. The patient's "I don't knows" seem reflexive. Her ensuing thoughts
may have been fruitful.

P: Well, I don't know what that is but, I mean, just. . .
A: Well. . .
P: . . .having this relationship. . .

A: But as if—yeah.
P: ...echo or something...
A: Right.
P: ...other relationship.
A: So the idea would be that, perhaps, as if: if I were to make
     an interpretation that somebody would say was a transfer-
     ence interpretation it would be—the reason that you feel I
     may not be strong enough to help you is because you are
     attributing to me the same lack of strength that your father
     showed when you asked him to help you with sex and he
     said, "I'm sorry, I can't..."
P: Mmm-hmm. "I really can't help you."
A: "I really can't." But you don't want to accept such an expla-
     nation and, in fact, you think it might be called superficial
     because it would wipe out all the things that happened last
     week that made you feel that I am not strong enough. Me,
     not your father.

Here the analyst seems to have captured her dilemma well: she
feels there is some connection with her father and yet she cannot
ignore the significance of her current feelings about the analyst.
The exchange captures a central idea in our view of transference—namely, that it always includes a plausible interpretation
by the patient of something in the present. Our emphasis on the
present—an emphasis that the therapist has clearly impressed
on the patient in this case—is a reaction against what we believe
to be the usual underemphasis on the present in favor of the
past. We do not deny the importance of the past, but we argue
for giving priority of attention—at least in terms of what has to
be dealt with first—to the present.

P: Right. But, you see— yes, but, but that— it is compli-
     cated. Right. [laugh] I mean, because...
A: Because you want to make it one or the other.

This reply seems to be too quick an effort to resolve the issue.
The patient should have been permitted to work it through
more thoroughly herself.

P: Probably. Yeah. Maybe that's it. Probably that's it. I think so.

A: Whereas, I think we have to consider the possibility that I
     did things last week that made you feel that I'm not strong
     enough, and that became assimilated to this feeling that
     your father wasn't strong enough, and the two of them to-
     gether combined to give you the experience of the relation-
     ship that you had and. . .
P: Mmm-hmm. Right.
A: I think, to be didactic with it for a moment, uh, it's true
     that what you said about your father could divert us from
     us. . .
P: Mmm-hmm.
A: That doesn't mean I don't want to hear those things when
     they occur to you. . .
P: Yeah. See. . .
A: But I now would like to continue and say — and what did I
     do last week that gave you the feeling that I'm not strong
     enough. My tiredness, perhaps, or other things?

The analyst does seem to be rushing her through to a resolution
which may turn out to be more imposed on her than integrated by
her. He also explicitly tells her he wants to hear the associations as
they occur to her. His misgivings about directing her rather than
exploring her feelings emerge in his calling himself "didactic." He
is indeed being so, perhaps characterologically, perhaps out of his
interest in this technical point, perhaps as an active defense
against the charge that he is not strong enough — probably all
three. He does, however, recover and manages to refocus attention on the thing that she may well have greatest difficulty verbalizing — her perceptions of his specific betrayals of weakness.

P: Maybe your tiredness. Although, you know. . .
A: That is to say, what you thought was tiredness.

As has happened repeatedly in the hour, a promising start in
exploring the patient's perceptions of the analyst is followed by
an abrupt, defensive and gratuitous emphasis on the subjectivi-
ty of the patient's impressions (compare p. 122, lines 2–7, with
p. 131, lines 25–29).

P: When I first noticed it — that's right. Right. I mean. . .

A: Yes.

P: That's right.

A: And what else?

P: I think you were—what else did we talk about last week? I think it had to do with this stuff about names, but if you ask me what else we talked about last week, I can't think of anything else.

A: And how did the thing about names make you feel that I'm not strong enough?

P: Uh. [slight pause] All right. I think it's the thing about names, but I think it's the thing about names on top of everything about money, and the thing about names that was also— it was that you hadn't remembered the way I remembered it. [pause]

A: But if I may so, so— that suggests. . .

P: I don't know. Yeah.

A: . . . that you are unquestionably correct.

P: Oh, yes. You're right. And I may be wrong.

A: But you are sufficiently sure that you are right that you're willing to conclude that my not remembering it correctly— quote, unquote—means that I'm not strong.

This appears to be a very charged counterattack. Presumably, he asked her to describe the cues that betrayed weakness in the spirit of eliciting even impressions she was not certain about. But, as he has done before, once she opens her mouth, he crosses her up and treats her like a witness in a court of law.

P: I don't, I don't know. I don't, I don't know where— because, you know, I mean, I can see where— I mean, I think I was disappointed that you hadn't. You know, that you. . .

A: That I hadn't what?

P: That you didn't think of me by my first name.

A: Didn't think of you? By your first name?

P: Well. . .

A: Now you substituted that for call you by your first name.

She is obviously flustered, and it is this which he should address. Instead, he continues with what is taking on the quality of an assault. Is he trying to prove to her how strong he really is?

P: Well [laugh], it simply turns out to be call me [?], you know. I mean, but you're right, they aren't the same. But I think of you as Dr. M and I call you Dr. M.

A: Yeah.

P: It's absolutely true that I think of— let's see, I'm sure there's some people—I can't think of any right now but I know there's people who I think of. . .

A: Perhaps, you feel that I'm afraid to think of you or to call you by your first name and that that's another indication of weakness on my part.

He interrupts her effort to justify herself. But he does make an interesting suggestion. Is it born out of his capacity to see her point of view or his interest in defending himself? Probably both.

P: I, you said also, you had—that you didn't know, you know. I mean, I told you now I would prefer you'd call me by my first name and you said— and then we'd have to look at that but. . .

A: Yes.

P: But you didn't know. . .

A: Which I would do.

P: Yes. Yeah. That's right.

A: And that's a sign of weakness. How is that?

P: Well. . .

A: Because I wasn't sure what I was going to do?

P: I don't— know.

A: What?

P: I don't know. Now I feel, the way I feel now is, is you're going to prove to me point by point— I have nothing. . .

A: Yes.

P: There's nothing, and I had absolutely no reason at all for me to feel that so. . .

A: That you had absolutely no reason to feel that I. . .

P: That's right. That it wasn't going well and that you weren't able to, to, to deal with me or to handle whatever I was saying or whatever.

Whatever the analyst's motives may be, there is no question that the patient is experiencing him as attacking her. The episode is an interesting miscarriage of one of the principles we espouse—namely, that the analysis of the transference should begin with an examination of the patient's experience of the relationship in the here-and-now, including a thorough exploration of the analyst's contribution from the patient's point of view. In this case, for example, the first task should be to help the patient articulate the evidence that he is not "strong enough" to deal with her. She may, for example, see him as a tired man, whose memory is failing him, who is not always aware of the time, who is very uncertain about many things, and whose weaknesses she is obliged to accommodate in some way. If it becomes clear that other interpretations of the present are possible, the way is open to look for how the patient's interpretation of the present, or her adaptation to that interpretation, has been shaped by the past. The miscarriage of the principle lies in the analyst's too quick and defensive attack on how she has construed the present—a reaction which, incidentally, the patient may register as confirmation of her impression of his weakness. And is this countertransference not a clue to the very reason the present is so often underemphasized in favor of the past?

A: And that's designed to make you look like a jackass.
P: Or feel that way anyway. [laugh]
A: Or feel that way. So you, you, you—I see. And that's because you behaved like a smart ass so I'm gonna show you you're a jackass. [patient laughs] Is that it? That could be the sequence.
P: Yeah.
A: That you feel this is my subtle way of putting you down for being a smart ass.

To his credit, it must be said he finally catches how she is experiencing his behavior. He suggests she may feel he is responding to her being a smart ass. Perhaps it is more specifically that she has impugned his power.

P: Yeah. But it's also just disconcerting because I—well, I mean—I think all the things you've said up to now, I mean, about the fears anyway, are fairly accurate expression of what the fears are, you know, and I guess, I don't want to keep the fears, you know. I do want them to be dispelled but, at the same time . . .

A: But at the same time, it's disconcerting to be told that you have manufactured this tissue of lies about me. Is that it?

P: [laughing] That's right. Yes. And also then I wonder where it comes from, you know. I mean, it's, I . . .

A: And to say it just comes from your father's difficulty in dealing with sex is superficial.

She has expressed the principle mentioned just above. How can she reconcile that she feels her fears are justified, that she wants them dispelled, and that she also wonders where they came from (i.e., the past)? The analyst does well here in empathizing with the patient's sense that he has been unwilling to take her perceptions of him seriously.

P: Well, I don't know if it's superficial or not. I mean, it's, it's superficial in the sense that just saying that doesn't—. Now, who knows why, you know, I mean, may be another set of problems in me and, you know, it probably is, but just saying that doesn't—yes, it doesn't say anything. It doesn't open up any doors.

A: Let me suggest another possibility. What? Saying that doesn't open anything. Yes.

P: Yeah. No.

The analyst's response here suggests he is listening with only one ear and heard her only on the "second take." He is too busy preparing his proposed resolution. And he is too ready to brush the past aside. What does she mean by "another set of problems"? The end of the session is approaching. Perhaps he feels some need for closure. But probably, more importantly, his in-

vestment in the issue — perhaps even in pushing the present as
against the past — is leading him to lose the focus on her experience in favor of his own constructions.

A: Let me suggest another possible way of looking at it: that
as we review what it was that made you feel that I'm too
weak to deal with you, we could see not that you didn't,
don't have a leg to stand on, but that, in the light of how
you were looking at things, it seemed plausible to you, but
that as we examine it very carefully, at least a number of
them don't stand up.

He has faltered. To say they don't stand up is to say her interpretation is *wrong*. But it is not wrong. It is rather that hers is
one plausible interpretation of the present but not the only possible one. He should leave open the possibility that she is "right"
too, and then explore what follows for her if, indeed, she is
right. Perhaps, concretely, he should explore what she has been
doing, in her thoughts and in her behavior, in response to her
perceptions of him.

P: Uh-huh. Uh-huh.
A: Uh, you say "yes." Do you see that as a different way of
looking at it from the fact that you just, uh, are deaf, dumb
and blind?
P: That you're showing me this...
A: What?
P: That, that there's another whole way of looking at it, right?
Is that right?
A: Yes. That there's another way of looking at it in part, and
in part I simply am not taking a position.
P: Mmm-hmm.
A: You said my eyes looked tired, let's take an example.
P: Mmm-hmm.
A: I, I haven't told you whether I think you were right or
wrong.
P: No.
A: But you're assuming that simply because I don't say "Yes,
you're right" and so on, that that means you were wrong.

P: Mmmmmm...
A: Right?
P: Mmm-hmm. I think.
A: It's almost as if you need for me to get a confirmation or —
     well, it's another example of the thing, uh — if I raise a
     question, you think I'm saying it's not so.
P: That's right. That's right.
A: Time is up.
P: Bye.
A: Bye.

Her formulation comes a little closer to a correct statement of
the principle as we see it and he moves toward accepting it. The
problem is that he is disclaiming something that he has been
saying or implying and blaming the patient. He is telling her, in
effect, that her sense that he wants to discredit her perceptions is
irrational. But, ironically, this repeats the very error he has
been making — that of jumping to question the validity of her
perceptions, instead of encouraging her to elaborate them.

Additional Comments

The faults of this session are intimately connected with its vir-
tues. The analyst's defensiveness emerges sharply as he attempts to explore aspects of the patient's experience of him
which he finds unpleasant to confront. His refusal, for example,
to be sidetracked by genetic material which might take him off
the hook of appearing not strong enough is embedded in an apparent assertion of his authority (strength) in his excessively didactic insistence on the priority of the here-and-now. Evidence
of the patient's compliance makes one all the more concerned
about the degree to which the analyst's activity may bespeak his
need to control the sessions. Yet, withal, the patient has been
helped to say some things that were probably quite difficult for
her to express. The working atmosphere seems good. We doubt
that there would have been comparable movement in a session
in which the analyst was largely silently listening to free associations, a session which might well have been much less subject to

criticism according to generally prevailing criteria of good technique.

In general, attempts to pursue plausible bases for transference ideas will bring up issues about which the analyst may be sensitive and to which he may react defensively. If he recovers and can explore the patient's experience of his defensiveness (during the session in which it occurs or in a subsequent one), the analyst may suffer some embarrassment, but the gains for the patient may be significant. The alternative is to make the prevention or concealment of countertransference of such paramount importance that it actually precludes a lively, collaborative exploration of the transference.

7

PATIENT G: SESSION 28

INTRODUCTION

This session illustrates commendable efforts by the therapist to clarify the patient's experience of the relationship and the therapist's contribution to it, as well as defensive maneuvers on both the patient's and the therapist's parts to depreciate the patient's perceptions. The therapist effectively focuses on a number of clues which could easily have been overlooked. At the same time, it is not easy to decide the correct order of importance of several different themes in the patient's experience of the relationship (a point that will be elaborated on in the comments following the session).

THE ANNOTATED SESSION

P: [short pause] Hi.
A: Good morning.
P: [pause] I guess I haven't communicated too well with my roommate—vice versa. Had a conversation last night—I don't know. Roommate is funny. He— feels I'm dependent on him. I'm the only person he's ever met who, I don't know, is not washing dishes and didn't understand how to make hamburger. I don't know. A funny kind of a conversation. It sort of cleared the air, but it didn't make me feel very good. It's so petty. I used the word "gosh" or "golly," I don't remember which. I pick up words. Didn't like my using Hebrew, which I have a tendency to use from time to time. Doesn't want me to use that word. I don't know.

A: Which word?

P: "Gosh"— "gosh" or "golly." I don't remember now which. He felt that showed dependency. It's just a word I use. I don't see it as having a, uh, great significance, you know. It's just an exclamation. Sometimes I use "wow." I don't know. I guess, some theory, you know, that it shows child- ish dependency or something. I don't know. It just hap- pens to be a word that I use. So he's giving me a warning not to use the word. I said, "OK. I won't use the word." Doesn't mean that much to me; I mean, it's not a primal word or anything. Uh, so I don't know. I just kinda feel funny about that. Sort of, you know—this happened last night—it did sort of, I guess, clear the air, but it's just hard to deal with, like—. I don't know. He doesn't have any compassion. I don't know. Just, uh—. Things just bother him. The way I do things ain't— it's hard for him to ex- press his feelings. Well, he hasn't told me. Well, I can't know what he's thinking if he doesn't tell me. I'm no, uh—. I don't have perception of the things he's gonna tell me. But I don't know. I guess it's just sort of discouraging, I guess; things may change. I may learn how to wash dishes or cook. I can't see where there are really blocks. I should be able to do that kind of stuff. It's just sort of discouraging; uh, when I first met him, I, we just seemed to have a lot in common. It's just that two people could talk well together but not necessarily live together or anything and it, it's awkward. It just seems [inaudible] awkward living with somebody when you're just sharing space and having noth- ing to do with them. It can be boring [yawn], lonely, what- ever word you want to use, living by yourself. And, I guess, there are other frustrations too. Most— I know a lot of people, I have a lot of friends, but even with my close friends, they don't bother to call, and I know these are things I've complained about before. I know some of the reasons and just the way they work at some things. They care about me, I know that, but they don't, you know, bother to pick up a phone and see if I'm alive or dead or what the hell I'm doing and, I guess, I'm just pissed off. Like a friend of mine who's in law school in S [another city].

She always said—well, you know, I don't write letters.
Well, I'm fed up. I think that's symptomatic of my friends,
they don't bother to write letters, call or, uh—or anything.
It just keeps going on. Some people— people are somewhat, I don't know, fairly dependable but, I don't know,
it's typical. Maybe I'm equating to my roommate, and
him, I don't know, he's just off in his dream world. I don't
know. Trying to solve his problems. I don't know. Bitching
on me to do this or that. I'm not that picky, like, you know.
He didn't throw away the garbage so I didn't, you know—I
care a little but I thought—he's human, he forgot to throw
away the garbage. He's supposed to throw away the garbage for May. That was his idea. So he apologized. He's
gonna throw it out for June. So I don't know. I don't know
how much it's me, how much it's other people. I don't
know. Part of me maybe, just like to— see, that whole big
— move to [?] desert island, uh; maybe I wouldn't get
along with the tree. I don't know if it's the jungle motif or
what. Uh, I don't know. Then I got a new job. I'm in the
beginning of a three-week training session which is really
boring. Some interesting people. Uh. . .

A: You say there are some interesting people?

P: Yeah. What's been interesting about it—it's been, well, a
couple of— there's, like, 30 people in the training session,
so yesterday I met somebody who has a Master's in English
literature from L University who's intelligent and, uh,
that's OK. I'm not even going to work with these—. Well,
I am working with him. I'll be in the same general area. I
don't know where they're gonna stick me. But there I train
until June 20th and I start June 23rd. Doesn't sound terribly exciting. It's knocking on people's doors that haven't
paid their taxes. Frankly, uh—. I don't know. Sort of drifting. Uh, I wrote a letter to my cousin. I just—I don't
know, there's no firm base. I guess my work has provided
that; Judaism provided that for awhile and then the sex
stuff [laugh], but, uh. . .

A: Your work and then Judaism and then sex?

P: Mmm-hmm. Yeah. Yeah. Free association. Uh. [slight
pause] If I even go into libraries, I sort of feel like a, uh—.

I don't know, a—. Here I am a city worker using a city agency and if I'm not patient, I get really bad service—FT [city-run institution]. Really understand— I can't get a job there. It's sort of displacement. I guess it's motif. Judaism, it's hard to tell, I use it for different reasons. Sex is hard to tell too. I feel [inaudible—lowers voice], I don't know. And there are changes. I'm an uncle now for the first time, as of two days ago. Although I have the nephew in M [another state] who I'll not see for, I guess, a month, but that's a new generation. Uh, my brother and sister-in-law are moving to town next week. I think I, I think I can get them a job at the census which I left.

A: Your brother and sister-in-law are coming. . .
P: I mean, from O [another city] to D [this city]. Yeah. He thinks he can be a doctor.
A: Wants to go to medical school.
P: Yeah. But he is quite [?] and has no medical background. He took very few science courses in college. Long shot. Yeah. Which is—. But he is determined. Uh—. I'm sort of drifting. I guess I will go to law school next year. I have to take LSAT and stuff. Uh. . .

The associations are rambling. The patient himself refers to his productions as drifting (p. 151, line 32), free association (p. 151, line 38), and now drifting again. The content carries a major theme of complaint about other people. There may be an allusion to a complaint about the therapist, for reasons we don't know, which takes the form of a kind of mockery of free association, with the implication that the therapist is responsible for allowing him to drift.

A: You have taken it, you say, or. . .
P: No. I have to take it. You really— it's given five times a year. I have to get it together and decide when I'm going to take it and take a [?] course and stuff. Uh—. I, I just don't know. Can I be the only person in the world that has a problem washing dishes? [laugh] It all sounds sort of ludicrous. It's certainly—. I don't know. Just felt on the defensive when we were talking about my problems last night. I

felt—but he was talking about things too. He didn't get too analytical about himself. He was talking about problems he had. I told him I thought he was judgmental and confusing and everything. I don't know. [pause] That's the image I've got, this funny sort of boat image, I guess, drifting on a boat, uh, between and betwixted or whatever. . .

A: Between what?

P: I just think of careers—. Maybe. I don't know. Uh, I guess I get some more connotations than that. Uh. [pause] That I've accomplished things. That I'll accomplish more things, uh—. I don't know. Try new things. I'm going to a thing to be a, uh— [whistle] uh, volunteer with A [organization] in V [suburb]. I can teach English—. Trying new things too. Uh—. I'm somewhat down on myself this week. I don't know. I'm just. . .

A: Down on yourself?

P: Yeah. I just— things frustrate me. I don't know. I've been working on a couple of jobs besides—and there's the synagogue job which is sort of around and, uh—. I did some— the census is almost over. I have one little thing left I forgot last night I think that'll be over today. I was helping a friend with some bookkeeping.

A: You were hoping to do what about. . .

P: I was helping a friend with some bookkeeping.

A: Oh, helping. I see.

P: That's over. Uh—. I don't know. It's, you know, it's sort of funny. I get down on myself and then I'm mad that I'm down on myself.

A: I don't quite know what you mean when you say you're down on yourself.

He may be scolding himself rather than scolding the therapist or he may be identifying, in his self-criticisms, with the response he thinks the therapist might have to his drifting.

P: Well, it— I can't find a check I got yesterday which [inaudible] wasn't very big and I just, you know, get mad that I do things like that, that I, that it looks like I may have lost a check. But it's frustrating, you know, just little things bother me, uh, I just— the key in the back door won't work —it's stuck in the back door. I just wrote a—. You get work orders—I wrote a work order to the janitor, which is all I can do, but I—why do these little dumb things happen to me? Why do keys get stuck in doors or whatever. Why do I —I probably left the check at work—why do I not take better care of a $45 check? Whatever. Little things that go wrong. [pause] And sometimes it seems that there's this air of loneliness around me, but it's not all the time. I don't know.

A: I'm sorry. You swallowed that word.

P: OK. They're funny things that seem to be around all the time; I'm not sure if they're around all the time at all. One is maybe an air of loneliness. I. . .

A: An air of loneliness.

P: Yeah. OK. One is that am I always that sexually alert. It really bothers me—am I always looking for a play, whatever? I don't know if I am or not, you know, always furtively looking on subway trains or something, uh, for people. Earrings in the left ear—that's a sign they're homosexual. I don't know. Or is that just passing the time or what? R [name] said that was just passing the time or what, what are the realities. Uh, I don't know. Uh. [pause] It's summer, but I don't know what that means. Uh, I don't— I'd like to be with somebody else. I don't know, just sharing time with someone, somebody [?], lover, I don't know. That doesn't seem to work either. Uh. . .

A: You guess, a lover, did you say?

P: Yeah.

A: Mmm-hmm.

P: [pause] I don't want to be alone the rest of my life. I really don't. [pause] When I, when I get down on myself, you know, I just think—well, maybe I haven't accomplished anything with you at all. I mean, I just get this—well, uh, a log——, it seems like a logical assumption somehow.

A: Down on yourself seems to mean scolding yourself or thinking. . .

P: Yeah. Just. . .

A: . . .ill of yourself.

P: You know, this thing of father figure. Yeah. You know.

A: A father...

P: Yeah. Assuming that I'm doing these things wrong and nothing is working and these things aren't happening to other people, they're just happening to me and, uh...

A: I didn't understand what you said about a father.

P: Well, just the idea of scolding, of finger pointing, whatever, uh, "you're a bad boy," whatever.

A: You mean, you're scolding yourself the way you imagine some father person would scold you?

P: Yeah. I guess maybe the way I imagine my father would scold me. Yeah.

A: And you said something about not having accomplished anything with me. Is that...?

This is the first explicit reference to the relationship the patient has made and the therapist focuses on it. Perhaps this is what the patient has been alluding to in his complaints up to this point: the therapy hasn't helped him.

P: Well, yeah. The context of that is — I think it's the jump — you talked about jumping — you know, well — jump — sort of a panic thing — whatever. Where you sort of leap — leapfrog — leapfrog from thought to thought. See, you can leapfrog from — well, you know...

His referring to "panic" and "leapfrogging" from thought to thought confirms the earlier speculation that his manner of associating has a meaning for his experience of the relationship, i.e., it is interpersonally motivated.

P: "You lost a $45 check — well, you're a bad person. Well, you're a bad person, you're a bad person before —." I can say, "Golly — you're still a bad person —." Well, I guess you're dealing —. We talked about that little problem. You're saying, "Dr. W has really not helped you," and I don't know. So then — we were just batting around this last week. I'm a failure, you're a failure —. I forgot what that connoted.

A: You forgot what?

P: What that connoted. Well, I guess it is, it is mostly guilt on my part, feeling guilty sort of that I have not availed myself of the gifts of Dr. W and his graduate seminar class.

A: Oh.

P: And I guess for that, you know, time is running out. The crystal ball with the sand ends July 21st.

The patient's anger surfaces in this biting sarcasm. We learn that the patient knows his sessions are being used for teaching and that a termination date looms ahead, associated, perhaps, with the ending of the class. His anger about both of these circumstances of the therapy is probably related to his anger about not having been helped, or at least not enough. He may feel that the circumstances have made it impossible for him to benefit from the therapy, or that he is being forced to terminate before he is ready. He attempts to avoid blaming the therapist by blaming himself.

A: So you mean, the way you're feeling now, makes you feel that, perhaps, you haven't gained anything in the therapy.

This comment understates the immediacy and intensity of the patient's anger. A retrospective interpretation may well be in order now, interpreting the earlier references to unsatisfactory relationships with people who don't extend themselves as alluding to the therapist's self-centered, impersonal, or exploitative purposes. In retrospect, the therapist's focusing (p. 155, line 13) on the patient's earlier remark about not having accomplished anything in therapy seems to have opened the floodgates.

P: I don't know. You see, it hits me once and awhile. I can't say it's pervasive. It's just maybe once and awhile. I don't know. I guess it's the feeling—you shouldn't, if you, if—. It's a theorem: if you've accomplished something with Dr. W, you shouldn't be feeling this way.

A: Mmm-hmm.

P: I don't know where that's coming from. Uh. . .

A: And I wasn't quite clear where the burden of the blame falls.

P: I don't know. We were tossing it around last week.

A: Yes. We were.

P: I guess, the burden is mine. I just can't, uh—. I don't have any, uh, theses to, uh— to pin on the wall against you. It just seems, you know—. You're, I guess, you've become some sort of a prop. I think it's, uh—. Well, let's, let's use —there are ten things we can use against G [patient's first name] and it's, like, fill in the blank and it's just—I don't know if I'm coming across. It's like, uh, I'm— it's more or less—not like it doesn't make any difference—more like I've got this mood-set, mind-set, whatever, that I'm mad at myself and what things can I do—what things can be imagined, exaggerated, whatever—that will fit into this mind-set, so it's like using events, maybe distorting events— using events—appropriating events that have no meaning or don't—or aren't really that—don't have that strong meaning. Using them into a certain framework. And maybe it's just stuffing my relationship with you into the framework. If the framework is: G is a bad person and a nebbish— whatever I'm, I'm terming myself as—well, I can use this relationship as one of my elements of that, uh—. The framework. [pause] It's funny talking to you now because I feel a little, a little sadness—not really terribly intense but fairly forthright, fairly sure of myself as I'm talking, and somehow getting it out seems to be somewhat, uh, encouraging and the more I think of, uh—. Last night's conversation, though, had its— was I think helpful. Like airing of these other things that I'm going through. I realized that— they aren't really that important. They may— maybe at 10:30 last night they seemed important or at 5:00, when a certain event happened, but even in the context of a certain day, it is not all that important. They're just sort of— it's all how you're painting it. They're not—they have meaning, I guess—but they're not so bad; they're really sort of just there and, uh, they don't—. They're just not all that important. They are just elements that happen to be going on. What's interesting is, I guess, what they're building blocks in the same way they can be used as building blocks or something. They can be used as building blocks for different world views or maybe just not — just building blocks that aren't part of the world views. The world views is just not part of that. Manage to be separate from that. You just — that I, I guess, carry a world view with me. [pause]

A: I think you have some feeling that I am disappointed in you or blaming you for. . .

Rather than go along with the patient and agree that he is construing everything in terms of his discouragement — in effect supporting his denial — the therapist stays with the patient's experience of the relationship. He chooses to interpret that the patient feels blamed by him rather than that the patient is blaming him, perhaps because the latter would be too painful to admit.

P: No. You're —. You're not —. You're just coming across kind of quiet today. [laugh] I don't know how you're coming across. Well, sort of — it's embarrassing, you know —. It's, uh —. It hurts, you know. I thought — I was telling B [roommate] last night — I thought we were going to break off May 23rd. I guess, maybe it just — I'll carry that with me in whatever conversations we have from now on, you know — just that I could have, should have, whatever — broken off then, but it, it hurts coming. I don't know why. I think it was a feeling of failure that we both agreed to that, you know. I'm still coming to you, you know — still needing the help, whatever. Other people don't, you know.

This is a good example of how the therapist's sticking to the patient's experience of the relationship enables the patient to reveal aspects of it he was resisting.

A: Are you suggesting that somehow I made you feel you had failed here by not, uh — ending it on May the 23rd? Is that what you're suggesting? That somehow you keep carrying that as a feeling that I have made a judgment that you haven't succeeded here?

P: [pause] I don't know what you think, uh —. I'm not sure how you enter into this —. Really into this. Uh —. I don't know. You see, I don't know the context of how often you see people or how long you see other people for or, uh, what your guidelines are, you know — I just know what I'm going through with you. [laugh] So I don't know how you — where I fit in or how you relate me. Uh, I don't know. Uh. . .

A: I understand that, but I think we're trying to clarify what you feel I feel — . Whether you could be certain of it or not.

P: I guess there's a feeling of — that I feel that you feel that I shouldn't be feeling the way I do.

A: Yes.

P: That if you had made a difference — that's the goal of the analyst — if you had made a difference, then I don't know why — I should be coming in on — springing sommersaults or something. I'm so happy.

A: Mmm-hmm. So you feel that I am disappointed, in you, and, possibly, even pointing the finger at you and saying you're a bad boy. If you had used this treatment the way you should have — you had this wonderful opportunity. . .

P: I'm smiling at your tone of voice.

A: What is there about the tone of voice?

P: It seems to change.

A: In what way?

P: There was more inflection; once your voice went somewhat higher. I don't know. It seemed different.

A: You mean when I said "you're a bad boy"?

P: Yeah.

A: When I was speaking for you.

P: Mmm-hmm.

A: You understood that. I was speaking — well, I was speaking the way I thought you would imagine I was feeling. Right? I don't quite understand why that made you smile.

P: [pause] Because you just seemed to say it with a different tone of voice.

A: Yes.

P: And tones seem to connote a different meaning, and I'm not sure what the meaning was.

A: What do you think it was?

P: Well, it came across as sort of role-playing.

A: And why would that make you smile?

P: Well, sometimes you seem sort of theatrical. I just— your tone of voice. I pick up things that you don't implicitly feel, think, whatever—. Smile a lot. Uh—. I can—you know, at certain times—I can do, I think, a fairly good Dr. W imitation.

A: Mmm-hmm.

P: If I, if the mood strikes. Uh. . .

A: And if I become theatrical, how does that lead you to smile? You take some— or what does that make you feel?

P: [pause] Well, I guess it's sort of a prop. I mean, I guess I see my laughing, whistling, hand motions as sort of a prop, and it seems like sort of a prop with you. It's part of your act or something. You're going, uh—. Your, your prop is not a—. You're always wearing a suit and tie so that's, you know, the uniform, but the prop is more the tone of voice that comes through.

A: What do you mean about the [inaudible]. . .

P: There's this more-or-less, uh—. When you want to make a point that you come to, your voice changes and you just sort of paraphrase and—you know, this is the thought for the day or something.

A: But why does that make you smile?

The continuing effort to make the patient's experience of the relationship explicit is noteworthy. The patient, however, may experience it as an interrogation; the therapist should be alert for this possibility.

P: I don't know. I guess I—. I guess I feel—. What came to my mind is a performing seal—apparently, I would be the performing seal—that I'm expected to clap or something, or I should even feel proud of myself that I caught the point, like, you're a professor and you've given me, you've expl—, you've gone to the punch line. This is a joke—this is the punch line. This is—. I'm supposed to show my appreciation, but I anticipate it. I'm happy with myself I've anticipated; I'm trying to show you my pleasure for the funny punch line. [pause]

A: I see. I think I see. You feel I'm sort of performing.

P: Yeah.

A: And as a performer, presumably, I would hope to have an appreciative audience...

P: Yeah.

A: And your smile is your effort to convey to me that you are being an appreciative audience. Is that correct?

P: Yeah. Well, who am I doing this lousy stuff for? All these impressions, who am I doing this for? [inaudible]

A: Well, it sounded as if that— if that analysis of the situation is correct, that you were doing it to please me.

P: Yes. [pause] Yeah.

A: The reason that that seems important to me is that I believe you do— feel a rather strong—. Or how shall I—? Let me say it this way—I think that your idea of what I'm feeling is very important to you. Uh, for instance, I think if you feel that I am disappointed in you or think you have failed in this therapy that that, uh, is something very distressing to you and, similarly, if you feel that I'm performing and would like to get a certain response from you, you very much want to give it to me. I think you— perhaps, I could, uh, summarize that by saying, I think it's exceedingly important to you to please me. I think even, uh, I could relate that to what you began with today. Obviously, you were very disappointed and very down and it seemed as if the central, uh, immediate thing that was moving you to feel that way was your disappointment in your relationship with your roommate. You entered that relationship with high hopes, I think, and, uh, apparently, they're not being realized. He is complaining, so...

P: No. He didn't. I had to mention this last night. He doesn't complain. It's hard for him to say what he thinks.

A: Well, but let us say, you feel his disapproval or disappointment.

P: No. It had to come up in the conversation when I mentioned something. Yeah. I feel it.

A: And that's very distressing to you and makes you feel very lonely. Uh, I think that was a, that's a correct assessment of what you were saying. The only point I'm trying to make right now is that I believe that, uh, your need and wish to please him and, and gratify him, seems to me, somewhat similar to the fact that you strongly wish to please and gratify me and are distressed if you feel that, uh, you are disappointing me or that the kind of bond that you had hoped for between us, you fear is not, uh, being fulfilled.

P: Well, I can agree with that until the bond part being fulfilled. I don't know. I don't know what that means.

A: [pause] Let me try to say that in a slightly different way. I think your sense of self-esteem rests very heavily on gaining my approval and that if you feel I'm disappointed, your own sense of self-esteem fails and another way — and one of the ways in which you try to gain my approval is to try to give me what you feel I want even if it's in such an apparently small thing as I perform by playing a role and you're supposed to [clapping sound] smile and clap. [pause] What did that shrug betoken?

The therapist's point is plausible and he has ridden it hard. But it is by no means the only plausible interpretation. For example, the therapist was so silent during the first part of the session that the patient remarked on it (p. 158). The patient's smile might therefore have been pleasure that the therapist was becoming more responsive. Moreover, while it is probably true that the patient wants the therapist's approval, what seems more immediate is the patient's amusement at the therapist's own need for approval, as shown in his grand-standing appeal for applause and narcissistic gratification. In line with this, what may well be more central than who is seeking approval is the patient's complaint that the therapy hasn't helped him and that it seems designed to gratify the therapist rather than to help the patient. Though the patient quickly identified himself as the trained seal, he explicitly indicated how he feels the therapist is performing too. Focusing on the patient's need for approval may not only serve as a deflection from the patient's feeling that the therapist needs approval but, more importantly, may obscure the patient's complaint that he is not being helped.

P: It's just sort of morbid. I don't know. [yawn] The more—

the further we go, the more unpleasant things I hear about myself. [pause]

A: You mean, that what I just said comes across to you as something unpleasant about you?

P: Yeah.

A: Could you explain that to me?

P: [pause] Well, I mean, it's really loads of fun. Last night — I have to sort of — in a way, I was wearing clothes but I just felt naked before B and he says, "Well, what do you see as your problem?" That's all I need; he's analyzing his problem. I gave him this spiel — . And I don't know — your spiel, my spiel. [sigh] Well, I'm a lonely person without — with low self-confidence — whatever. It's just the same damn thing you were saying about the approval, so I just come here and get reinforcement, and I don't actually even feel that bad, but you get to tell me how bad I'm feeling, which makes me feel really good and, uh, then you just get to dissect things, and the way it comes across to me is I look bad and I guess I — . You know, I'm smiling and I shouldn't be smiling. I don't know that the only, the only thing that's important is your approval. I'm desperately — here's this poor kid, desperately looking for approval from his psychiatrist. And he can't get it, no matter what he does. It seems whatever I do is wrong, but you, you feel you're not being judgmental. I see it as judgmental. You feel you're not giving me criticism; I feel it as criticism. So what am I supposed to do? What's considered appropriate? I don't know. [pause]

He has plausibly experienced the interpretation as an insensitively administered narcissistic wound — primarily a criticism, rather than an empathic suggestion. His experience may be that the therapist not only does not recognize that he feels he has not been helped but indeed keeps emphasizing what is wrong with him.

A: So you essentially experienced what I had to say as putting you down.

The therapist neither defends himself nor apologizes but makes explicit his understanding of the patient's experience. What is missing, however, is what was emphasized so strongly in Volume I: the therapist fails to look for what in his own behavior makes the patient's experience plausible. On the contrary, he leaves the impression that the patient may have no "legitimate" basis for feeling as he does. The therapist also does not recognize that the patient's immediate complaint may be a displacement from the more basic complaint that he hasn't been helped.

P: I guess so. I feel sort of fed-up. I just get hard questions. I just misinterpret. I just feel. . .

A: Oh, I keep telling you there's something wrong with you.

P: I don't know. I mean —. Yeah, I guess. I just don't know. Partly what I'm feeling is I just come and find some new, some new disease or something. Some new, uh —. Something is wrong with me or, uh —. I think it's — think — something I think I think is wrong with me. Maybe just saying that is sort of a defense mechanism too. I. . .

A: How do you, how do you. . . ?

P: I, I don't know.

A: How do you mean a defense. . . ?

P: I don't know what I mean. [pause]

A: And have you some, uh, feeling of what my motive is in putting you down this way? Why, why did you laugh at that?

P: Because it doesn't make sense. What motive could you have in putting me down?

Is the therapist attempting to abort the patient's anger by quickly focusing on his saying he may be defending himself? While it is often useful to explore the patient's ideas about the analyst's motivations, here the inquiry may come across as suggesting that the analyst's having such a motive is so unlikely that the patient's experience must be unjustified. The patient's response suggests that he heard the therapist's question as: How could you possibly think such a ridiculous thought?

A: I don't know. But it seems to me that, I can understand that you essentially experience me as putting you down, so, presumably, you must feel I have a purpose in doing that.

That he says you "essentially experience me" suggests, again, a hyperbole — that there is no basis for the patient's feeling. This disguise of an attack as empathy makes it all the more difficult for the patient to assert his anger. Even so, he does in his next remark.

P: [pause] I feel pretty mad at you. Uh. . .
A: Yes. You sound irritated. Can you explain it to me?
P: [pause] I want some support. I don't get any. All I get is you want constant anal — , analysis of why this, why that. I don't know why. I have to scrounge around for reasons. I have to analyze all these things. I'm not good at analysis — at this kind of analysis. I'm just tired of your interpretations and being constantly asked to interpret this and to interpret that. I'm tired of playing the game.
A: [pause] So there's something about the whole way I'm doing, I'm conducting myself that you dislike and object to.

Now the therapist begins to search in a more neutral and receptive way for his contribution to the patient's experience.

P: I guess so. At other times, I guess I said I was happy with it and I thought I did — satisfied. I don't know. I'm just tired of the hard work. I'm tired of constantly — the constant dissecting.
A: Oh, you know, you mentioned that the other day, and I wasn't quite clear. You said this is too hard work.
P: Yeah. It's been bothering me.
A: What do you mean by that?
P: [pause] I'm not quite sure. I'm not sure if that means some sort of a reward, like, expect ice cream, or I expect just simple multiple-choice questions that are easier to grasp, or what, uh, or I expect some sort of different kind of meaning, or I expect something that I don't see as a criticism. I don't know. I'm really not sure.

The patient's self-recriminations are defensive at this point in that they absolve the therapist of blame. This is a common form of resistance to the awareness of negative feelings in the relationship.

A: [pause] Mmm-hmm. I would like to make a suggestion about it. Uh, you have, on a number of occasions, likened our interaction to a competition.
P: Yeah. I quit. I lost.
A: Uh, you lost.
P: Yeah.
A: What do you mean?

The therapist interrupts what he was going to say to follow the patient's experience.

P: I guess you're stronger than I am. You have a better, uh — . With background in analysis — a better understanding of these problems — whatever — than I do. I just seem to muddle things. I just seem to get confused.
A: Well, that's related...
P: I just seem to take everything as a criticism.
A: That's related to the point that I was going to make. You have spoken of my double-jumping and so on, and I was wondering whether the sense of hard work...
P: For what?

The therapist resumes his point since the patient's experience is a further expression of what he had in mind. The patient interjects a sarcastic remark — "For what?" — meaning his hard work is to no purpose. But the therapist continues, not recognizing that the reference may be to the patient's complaint about not being helped.

A: ...means that you're trying very hard in this competition to keep up with me and best me, or at least be even with me, but have the feeling that, uh, I have defeated you — as you just said — and, uh, it seems to me that that could lead to an answer to the question I asked a little while ago, as to what you feel my motive is. I think it's possible that you see me — why are you looking at the time?

P: I have to get going eventually and get back to class.

A: But why just now?

P: I want to go. I hoped it was time to go.

A: You what?

P: I guess I wanted to go. I hoped it was time to go.

A: You didn't want to hear what I had to say, perhaps...

This sounds a bit retaliatory. More important, however, is that the interaction between the two seems to reflect the content of the interpretation accurately. The therapist is trying to gain control of the situation by an interpretation and the patient is fighting back by attempting to ignore him. The therapist does well in stopping to address the nonverbal communication.

P: It could come across that way.

A: I'm sorry. What did you say?

P: It could come across that way. I don't remember feeling this angry with you. I'm not sure why.

A: Yes. Uh —. And I think, uh...

P: I mean, all you do, you're dissecting. You get to sit in the chair. I have to go out and be with myself 23 hours a day. [near tears]

A: Yes. I think that — and that's, apparently, what you feel is my, my motivation, that I just want to cut you up and, uh, that that's the competition almost — that I'm trying to cut you up and you're attempting to, uh, keep up with me in that game or something but feel that it's an unfair competition and that I'm, uh, essentially mistreating you. In fact, it occurs to me to consider that maybe you felt that, uh, I wanted to keep you after there had been kind of an agreement that you would leave because I wasn't through cutting you up yet, as it were. That I enjoy it somehow.

One could question whether this is really the patient's main point. The therapist may be revealing his distress at the patient's attack by making it an accusation of sadism — something that he can demonstrate is less justified and hence is easier to defend himself against than what the patient is really accusing him of.

The patient's criticism seems to stem more from his perception of the therapist's failure to help, a failure the patient may attribute to the therapist's narcissism, exhibitionism, and competitiveness, but probably not to his "sadism."

The therapist began to explore what there was in his behavior which was eliciting this attack by the patient, but he falters by, in part, overstating and, in part, inadequately stating the patient's complaint. The overstatement and misstatement of what the patient has complained about make the therapist's interpretation defensive in its overall effect.

P: Well, it gets very sticky. The question is: Why do I do this? Do I enjoy being cut up?

A: Why do you do what? Why did you...?

P: Why do I keep coming here? Why did I agree to come until the middle of July?

A: [pause] You do very much want to please me, I think.

The therapist returns to his major interpretation, apparently neither deterred by, nor much the wiser for, the patient's outburst.

P: What do I get out of it?

A: [pause] Just cut up.

P: [pause] I just feel, I feel I have this need now to just quit — failure, whatever — say the hell with it. Why bother?

A: I didn't hear the word "need" there. What did you say? "I feel..."

P: [sigh] I just feel like quitting, giving up — why, why bother going on? Whatever that means. Uh...

A: Mmm-hmm. [pause] Do you think you can say why you are so especially discouraged right now?

P: I feel sort of worse than I did when I walked in. Uh...

A: You mean, today?

P: Yeah. Today. [slight pause] I feel very feisty and argumentative, which I usually don't — usually I just feel relaxed at the end of the hour. I go out whistling. That's the trademark. Uh, I don't feel like whistling. Uh, I just feel I failed. [yawn] I mean, I just — you've got all the cards and you can go on and you'll take next year—whoever is sitting here next year being taped every week—your new patient, uh. . .

While it is clear that the patient is upset about the impending termination, it is good that the therapist does not attempt to explain his anger strictly on that basis, as that would be to overlook what has happened in the session. At the same time, what may be the more basic complaint is not being made explicit.

A: You have failed and I have all the cards. I don't quite understand what you mean by that. As if. . .

P: Goddamit. I don't know. I just—. I guess I don't know how to live. I don't know. I mean, you're a psychiatrist. You do your thing, I guess, whatever—you've coped. I don't know, I just haven't made it. [pause]

A: You mean, you feel inferior vis-à-vis me?

P: I guess so. I don't know if it's the comparison or what. [pause]

A: Well, that, it seems to me, does suggest that. . .

P: Well, it goes back to the metaphor of competition again. Yeah.

A: Yes.

P: Except that it's sort of st——. I'm trying to understand why people go to psychiatrists if they're trying to become a psychiatrist themselves or what they're trying to accomplish if they're competing against the psychiatrist. It's strange. I mean, theoretically, you're going to someone to work for something to serve needs, whatever, uh—. I don't know.

A: Well, I suppose you go for a variety of needs.

P: Yeah.

A: But it just would seem that one of the important ones is for you to— that you have experienced my behavior as an, as my effort to, uh, be victorious in this competition between us.

The therapist apparently began to interpret that the patient was motivated by a need to fail in a competition with the therapist but stopped himself, correctly recognizing that this would have been to put the onus on the patient. Instead, he more neutrally interprets the patient's experience of the relationship, leaving open who is to "blame."

P: Then it's too late to do anything. What's the use of going on at all? I mean, what are we gonna do? What are we gonna accomplish between now and July that we haven't experienced since October?

At this point the patient is so angry that he experiences every interpretation as an enactment of the competition. Even interpretations that are about that very thing are experienced as aloof, one-upmanship. There is little the therapist can do at such a juncture other than to point this out, since he is apparently unable to confront the accusation that the therapy has been a failure, or perhaps because the impending termination is a reality which cannot be changed.

A: You mean, if that is a correct...
P: If that's it, that's it. What are we gonna do from here?
A: [pause] It isn't entirely clear to me why if that's it, that raises the question of what shall we do now. What do you mean by that?
P: [some sort of movement] [sigh] If that is how it's been interpreted from somewhere within the analysis until now, then the analysis is not serving a purpose, the analysis is distorted. It hasn't worked. If it hasn't worked from that time until now, it's questionable what can be done with it from now until the end.
A: Mmm-hmm. Yes.
P: And you just come across so goddamned dispassionately and just ask these probing questions and I'm stuck coming up with answers — whatever I'm supposed to be coming up with — getting more confused even in my questions.

The therapist's apparent calm in the face of the storm is also a kind of victory — or does the patient feel it as a lack of responsiveness?

A: Mmm-hmm. So even my — not even — but my saying that

you have experienced it as a competition in which I am besting you is yet another move in this game of besting you. I'm showing you how rotten you are and how you misunderstood the whole goddamn thing, and because of this false construction that you have made of the therapy, it hasn't been worth a good goddamn and so why go on and just do more of the same.

This seems to be a much more accurate understanding of how the patient experienced the earlier interpretation (p. 169, lines 30–33). It is also noteworthy in that it includes a specification of how the therapist has contributed to the experience.

P: OK. There I'm confused because that's coming out of a framework, 'cause that seems to be coming out of a framework where here, again, it's not important what you say — if the framework is more important than the parts and it's working out of the framework that the therapy is wrong and sort of just— it's sort of—I can't win. I'm just using any—damn it—it's just that I'm using any, uh—. It's sort of a distorting of reality—not distorting of reality—it's just distorting things for your own purpose. It's not in the purpose of looking at things objectively. It's very passionately, objectively looking at things that fit into the framework. It's twisting squares into circles or whatever.

The patient apparently cannot accept the opening he has been given to blame the therapist, at least in part. He retreats to blaming himself for "distorting reality."

A: Are you speaking of what you think you may be doing?
P: Yeah.
A: And can you explain to me what is the context into which you are twisting things—as you see it?

The therapist seems too ready to accept what may be the patient's backing away from his anger.

P: [sigh]

A: That...

P: Yeah. I think I can. It's not gonna help me once I walk out the door, but it's some sort of rationale that I am a bad person, that I did not get anything through therapy, or that, uh, the world is rotten and I'm a terrible person that should die, or some derivation of that theme—some pessimistic, depressive, whatever theme.

A: That's one of the themes. But another one is that you're very angry with me and feel that I am, uh, mistreating you and not doing what you would want me to do. Instead of supporting you and helping you, I'm dissecting you and attempting to show you how rotten you are.

The therapist does bring the patient's anger back into focus, but the anger is attributed to the idea that the patient feels his faults are being dissected, rather than to the failure of the therapy or the termination.

P: [pause] It's hard to sort out. I mean we've gone through this, this whole struggle, whatever, of supportive and can it be supportive and, uh, if supportive can be one extreme, certainly dissect is another extreme. And interpretations, certainly there are different interpretations in the, in the middle, uh, and it just hurts a lot. I mean, the money doesn't mean much. I can write another check but it hurts a lot that I spent this much effort for nothing. I mean if not for nothing, this much effort and I can't— we, we— I, I haven't been helped that much. It hurts a lot.

A: The money—did you refer to the money you spent on this treatment?

P: Yeah. Whatever. But the emotional thing seems to hurt worse. I don't know. And the other thing is always—yeah, but where do we go from here? If I'm this angry, have I been angry with you all the time? If there's this competitiveness, then maybe it's something else that's never been dealt with.

A: Yes.

P: Yes. What the hell do I do?

A: Are you, perhaps, also concerned about how you think I am reacting to this? Uh. . .

While this may be an important theme, it seems to be a deflection from the patient's idea that the whole therapy may have been useless, or at least has left a great deal undealt with.

P: Yeah. I wonder if I'll feel guilty afterwards. Will I want to call you because I'm embarrassed that I was mean or whatever I was?

A: Yeah.

P: That I cannot look you in the eye or whatever.

A: You mean, you feel that I'm responding in a particular way to your being angry with me?

P: I don't know. No. I don't know how you're responding. You've got— your mode of question and tone of voice and everything else seems to be typical Dr. W, uh. . .

A: Which is what?

P: It's hard to pin down sometimes. Uh—. Lot of probing questions. Hard questions. I don't know. To me, a lot of change of voice and whatever.

A: What do you see. . .?

P: No answers. I guess I just want an answer once in awhile. Maybe, on one level, I want you to give me all the answers, whatever that means at this point in time. Like, I never get answers at all. I don't know. I'm coming in to a Delphic oracle; I never get any answers at all. I just have to try to interpret, sort out whatever I was, got myself stuck in [?] during the sessions, figure out something for myself. And I don't know, there have just been interpretations. One is that I just didn't meld that well with you or that. . .

A: You said what?

P: My behavior didn't meld that well [yawning] with your, uh, psychoanalytic treatment or, I don't know—. Or that I'm untreatable. I don't know. There are a lot of possibilities.

A: And do you feel that I share your, uh, view of the treatment—that it has been a failure and so on?

The therapist recognizes that the patient feels the whole treatment may have been a failure, but instead of simply verbalizing this understanding of the patient's position, he asks whether the patient thinks he agrees with him — thereby indirectly suggesting that in fact he does not agree. He is apparently reluctant to say that he does not agree — perhaps because, in principle, he believes he should not express a direct opinion; perhaps because he fears that if he does say so, this would only incite the patient to challenge him to prove it.

P: That's a hard question. How am I supposed to know if you share — ? You come across — it's — I can't tell how you come across because I get, uh —. A smile once in awhile. But you come across just as this barrier that you put up, that you're always calm and cool Dr. W. So it's hard to tell.

A: I understand that. But I'm asking you what you think I'm feeling behind this calm and cool exterior.

The therapist rightly refuses to stop with the patient's perceptions of his outward behavior.

P: I don't know. I don't know. I guess it hurts that I don't know. That I have no idea.

A: Mmm-hmm. You feel, for instance, that I resent your being angry with me? Think you...

The therapist seems to ignore the patient's saying that it hurts that he is so opaque, presumably because he is pursuing the line of thought he himself opened shortly before.

P: Well, I assume anyone resents my being angry with me, so I can't see that I'm particularly picking on you. I just see this problem dealing with anger and assume that you'll just assume, that you'll just — I'm looking for approval and I'm afraid of anger.

A: But you did say that you thought that you might feel guilty later and feel that you had been mean to me...

The therapist either didn't hear or is ignoring the patient's slip — "my being angry with me."

P: Yes. I had a flash of that. Yes.

A: . . .and want to call up and what?

P: Apologize, I guess.

A: Apologize. In other words, you feel that I may feel that you have behaved in a way that warrants an apology.

P: Yeah. [pause] And the damn thing is that we end—not right now—but everything just ends as gray as it's always been. That, I don't know, it seems, in a way, from square one—I don't know what you, I don't know what I want from you. I don't know what—I have no idea. It seems like an outburst. Last week, I was maybe more muddled but I guess that's maybe. . .

A: You have no idea about what?

P: [sigh] What my anger meant. What it symbolized to me or even to you or anything else. Where it's coming from. Where it's going to. Who it was directed at. Whether it portends anything for the future or the past or whatever.

A: Yes. I agree with you that some of those questions are— what was that?

P: How can you say I agree with you?

A: What do you mean?

P: I guess I want you to disagree with me. And not just come across as such a flat— "I agree with you," like just, just slapping me in the face.

The therapist's apparent calm and his not revealing his own position and feelings do seem to be making the patient very angry.

A: I hadn't. . .

P: No. I didn't give you any chance.

A: I hadn't finished saying what. . .

P: I cut you off at the beginning.

A: . . .I agree with you about, but tell me what, what did you think I was, was saying. Wha— wha— . . .

P: Well, I thought you were just being simplistic, and I had tried to come across with something and rather than your considering the issues, it came across as your just sort of flatly— "I agree with you."

A: I see. You mean, the issues—the ones that you have just expressed about this distress—uh, "I have this anger but I don't know where it's from, I don't know where it's going, I don't know what it means" and so on. And instead of my seriously taking the fact that you had all those questions, I said, "I agree with you," as if it was some sort of a, a stupid, simplistic flat dismissal of you. Is that how you...?

P: It came across as a dismissal. Yeah.

The therapist does seem to be empathically grasping the patient's experience.

A: Yes. Well, perhaps, I should finish my sentence. I was going to say with you, that I agree with you that there are all these questions that are unanswered and remain difficult bristling questions. That's what I was going to say.

P: But that's where I'm confused, because I was thinking you're supposed to keep going to a psychiatrist to get these questions answered, or am I supposed to answer all these questions myself? Or—. How do I decide what's answerable and what's unanswerable?

A: Yes. Well, all I can say to that is that we'll continue to do our best to find out what answers we can in what time we have. But, uh, I realize that's not a very satisfactory reply either.

P: [pause] Well, I don't—satisfactory is hard to say. Uh, I don't think you have a— a elephant up your sleeve. I don't know. [pause]

A: Yes. I think, however, that, uh, I would at least like to point out that, uh, I believe you think I share your view that if it's true that one of your motives has been to see this as a competition and, and that you feel that in this competition my behavior has been such as to be victorious and that you're a failure, that you think—well, you said that that would mean that, uh, the treatment had been useless and a failure and why go on with it—and I suspect that you feel that I share that view, and I'm just, uh, saying that's open to question. [pause] Why did that make you smile?

Again, it is fairly clear that the therapist wants to say he disagrees that the therapy has been a failure but feels he shouldn't say that directly.

P: 'Cause you come across strong and then you just end in the middle. I, you give a point of view and then say it's open to question.
A: That's right.
P: I mean, it's— you've always— I mean, this will be continued next week.
A: Right.
P: There's not always a next week.

The patient understands that the therapist is hinting that the treatment has not failed in his opinion. But from the patient's point of view termination is approaching and the therapy has failed. Perhaps the patient's emphasis on the failure of the therapy is designed to make the therapist feel guilty about the termination.

A: No. There isn't always, but there is now. And what is our time for next week?

Not a very satisfactory answer, but the therapist is apparently unwilling to consider continuing beyond the predetermined time for ending the therapy.

P: Well, this week I got out by saying I had a doctor's appointment, which was true. I don't know if that's gonna work next week. Is it possible around lunch? I think I've got a— they give you long lunches. One way out would be for me to just take a long lunch and come in late or something. Otherwise, I don't know. You see, they're 8:30 until 5:00 and they might be picky. I have two teachers I don't know. I missed the first week because I didn't bother to start until a week late.
A: What do you mean by lunch?
P: Lunch in present parlance is 11:45 until 1:00 from downtown.
A: Yeah. I could see you—. I could see you on Thursday at,

uh—. Oh, I think I have a cancellation—. What time could you get here? On Thursday?

P: Mmmmm. Depends on how the buses run. Uh. 12:10.

A: So if we met at 12:10, uh, we would finish at 1:00.

P: Yeah.

A: That's OK. All right?

P: I don't know if it's OK. I'll try to work something out. They keep— they're not—. I've had two different teachers. I don't know what's going on. We have experts come in. We can try that. Let me—. If you don't mind, let me play that by ear. By Monday or Tuesday, see if I know more about what's going on with the class and what they've got up their sleeve.

A: You want to phone me?

P: Sure, if something comes up, I'll phone you.

A: I mean, shall we make it for that time?

P: Yes. Let's make it for that time and I'll phone you if some problem comes up.

A: You'll phone me if there's a problem. So the time is, uh, Thursday at 12:10.

The therapist is being flexible about the appointment time. The patient's situation seems to warrant that—or is the therapist attempting to mollify him?

P: Well.—. Yeah. That's right. All that's on my mind now is your last—. And that is open to question—it's so ambiguous, uh. . .

A: All I mean by that is that you shouldn't take it for granted that I share your view.

P: But can I take anything for granted?

A: [pause] My. . .

P: No. I'm baiting you. [laugh]

A somewhat surprising but welcome insight. It undoubtedly provides relief to the therapist, and perhaps is intended by the patient to do just that.

A: Uh, you think you're baiting me?

P: Yeah.

A: Uh-huh. Well, all I — no, the next appointment would be 6, 12.

P: The 12th.

A: All I intended to say is that my, uh, purpose is to help clarify your thoughts as much as possible. Not to express my opinion. That's right.

P: OK. Bye.

A: Bye.

ADDITIONAL COMMENTS

As we studied this session we changed our minds several times about the relative importance of the several themes in the patient's experience of the relationship. At one point we believed the main theme was the patient's attribution of narcissism and exhibitionism to the therapist. Later, we believed that what was more central was the idea that the therapy had been a failure. But still later, we concluded that the patient's primary complaint was that the therapy was terminating prematurely. Doubtless these themes are related. One possible way of organizing them is to see the patient's complaint that the therapy has been a failure as a way of protesting that it is being terminated arbitrarily and too soon. Perhaps the patient stresses the alleged failure of the therapy in order to stimulate the therapist's guilt about the termination. The accusation of narcissism and exhibitionism may be reasons the patient is offering for the failure to be helped and for the forced termination. Readers may well organize the data in yet other ways.

The therapist seems to find it difficult to focus consistently on any of the themes we have proposed. The reason may be not only that the complaints are unpleasant to confront but also that he feels guilty about having set up the therapy, to a significant degree, for his own purposes.

At the end, the therapist seems concerned not to let the patient leave believing the therapist agrees with him that the therapy has been a failure. He seems caught between his wish to say this directly to reassure the patient (and perhaps himself) and

his belief that this would violate the principle of confining himself to exploring the patient's experience. The patient responds
with a sense of frustration and anger at not being able to shake
the therapist's clinical posture.

8

PATIENT H: SESSION 19

INTRODUCTION

In this session there is a dramatic shift from an apparently humdrum, unproductive process to a vivid and useful one when the therapist insists on exploring the meaning in the transference of a cancellation by the patient. Probably flushed by success, and perhaps because he has been restraining himself (one interpretation speaks of the patient's habit of reciting unimportant details), the therapist becomes overambitious. He leaves the transference and proposes both extra-transference and genetic interpretations, probably at the expense of further progress. Moreover, in his overactivity he may well contribute to a reenactment of a conflict-ridden experience from the patient's past.

THE ANNOTATED SESSION

P: [short pause] I don't know if this is right. I think I lost the bill.

A: Mmm. [pause] OK. I don't —. Well, I have to check.

P: OK.

A: All right. [pause] Which I will — I'll just — if it is not right, we'll just change the next one, you know, to adjust it.

P: Yeah. Last week, when I was supposed to come — just about 20 minutes before I was leaving to come here — my boss came over and —. They've just changed over companies and this was the final thing — all paperwork and everything. So C that I work with didn't come in. So he came

181

over and said— he handed me a big printout and says, "This gotta be done." I said, "All right. No problem." And I say—and I says, "Well, when do you need it by?" And he says, "Today." And I says, "Well, I've got 20 minutes— how's that, you know?" And he says, "I really need it today." So I went over to this other girl and asked her if, uh, she had anything that she had to do. I says, uh, "I'll start it, can you finish it?" And she says, "Well, I do have this." So I went back to him and I says, "Does this really have to be done today?" And he says, "I'd really like it." I says, "Well, you know, I leave—." I says, "There's nobody else here." I says, "If it has to be done, I'll stay." He said, "Well, if you would." I says, "OK." So I felt, in a way, I was doing him a little bit of a favor—not much, you know.

A: Did he know that you, uh, that you had an appointment?
P: Yeah. So I felt like, in a way, that I was doing him a favor.

Surely the therapist has heard "a little bit of a favor" as indicating that giving up her therapy session did not mean much to her. But, because he has in mind that perhaps she meant it was a small favor from the boss' point of view, he asks whether the boss knew about the appointment.

P: He came over and he says— this was about a quarter to five —he says, "Did you finish this?" I said, "No. I've got a few pages left." I said, "I'll have it done in the morning." And, I guess, somebody had gotten on his back about something and he said, "I told you you should have had this done to-day." And I says, you know, "I'm doing what I could." He says, "Well, I guess, you should stay overtime." And I says, "Oh, no. I did already stay overtime." I said, "I put aside an appointment that I have every week." I said, "And this is it." I said, "You know, I really—five o'clock, 40 hours." I said, "You know, not today." I said, "I'll. . .
A: What do you mean, five o'clock, 40 hours?
P: He said it, like—you should stay overtime.
A: Right.
P: And I said, "You can't insist on overtime."
A: But from his point of view—five o'clock is when you should

— he's doing you a favor to let you go at four, isn't that right?

P: No. I was saying to him, five o'clock means 40 hours a week...

A: I see.

P: ...and that's what a work week is. And I said, "There's not much left, you know." There—everybody was going home. Who was he gonna turn it in to?

A: Mmm-hmm.

P: And I says, "I'll have it done, you know, first thing in the morning." And he just stood there and he just started waving his hands and walked away and said, "Yeah. That's all right." And, uh, so the next morning, I came in and I finished it. I had it done, like, in a half-hour so I handed it back to him, and he says, "You know, hey, thanks a lot." And he says, "I'm sorry I blew up at you like that." And I says, "You know, I know what—." I says, "Everybody in this place is turning around in circles. Nobody knows what they're doing. They're making up new rules to this system as they go along and five people have their hands in one thing and they just keep changing it." So—. It was Thursday.

A: What do you mean, what did you mean by that—that everybody is making up new rules as they go along—in relation to what had happened?

P: Well, no, uh, just one person will come and if you ask them how something is to be done, they'll say This is it. Another person will come along and say, "Well, I'm higher up than him. This is how it really should be done." And you sit there and say, "Well, fine. OK. Sounds good." Another one will come along and say, "No. This is it." And you know, we're sitting there so, like, throughout every department that's about how it is, and I've asked, you know, my boss—I said, "What is going on here? You know, how come they have all kinds of different books and things of rules for that and it seems like nobody is following it." And I says, "It's just like everybody's at each other's throat, you know." He was, he was the tops, because he goes out to lunch and he has, like, a three-, four-hour lunch and he drinks, you know, the whole time and he comes back and he'll be called into one of the bigger guy's office and they'll start on him about something and he'll come back to our department and take on each one of us. Like Thursday, after lunch, he came back and I was standing there and he says, "What are you doing with jeans on today?" He said, "I ought to send you home." I said, "Well—." I says, "This isn't the first time I've worn jeans." He said, "But you shouldn't." And I says, "All right." I says, "Are you sending me home?" And he says, "No." And I says, "Is this a dress code?" And he says, "Don't wear jeans again." I says, "Oh, all right." And he came back and he said that to be sent home would be without pay. And I says, "Well, I don't make much anyhow so it's not gonna hurt me." And he— I was laughing—and he says, "And don't laugh." And I just left and I said, "All right." You know, go sit down and don't say anything to him, 'cause I knew that he would right away go crazy.

A possible speculation is that the associations about the unreasonable boss who demands conformity to rules are an allusion to the therapist, who the patient may think is unreasonably angry because she has violated the rule of regular attendance.

A: Mmm-hmm.
P: So this other guy that he works with came back and he says, "In about two minutes, I'm gonna punch this guy out." And I said, "Why don't you ask him what's bothering him?" I said, "Is it something about us? Is it somebody else?" You know. I said, "He's really gettin' down on all these different people." So he said, "Well, I'll take him out today for dinner and we'll talk about it." So they went out and Friday, they came back and I says, you know, "You find out what's buggin' him?" And he says, "No. Just leave him alone." So I sat there and every time I looked at him, my stomach would turn and it was like: "please, don't come near me 'cause I know you're not gonna have anything good to say and I'm just sitting here, you know—forget it, I'm staying away from you." So Friday, that's how the whole

day was. Everybody just sat there waiting for him to come by. So I says, "OK. I'm not gonna bother with him." So he comes by, later in the afternoon, again, and I says, "How was your lunch?" "It was all right. I didn't have enough to drink." And I says, "Oh, you know, well—." So he walked away and he comes back and he was talking to some guy. He says, "I think opening a gas station would be better business than this." And this guy says, "No. How about a lounge?" And I said, 'Yeah. That's a good idea." He says, "Yeah. She could be our bartender there." And he looked and he said, "What? You can't be a bartender; you're not old enough." And I said, "Yes I am." He said, "You gotta be at least 19." And I says, "I am at least 19." And I says— he says, "You're only 20." And I says, "No. You're wrong." I says, "I'm 23." He says, "Your nose!" I said, "I'm 23 years old." He says, "According to my records, when you applied here, you were 20 years old." And I said, "Well, let me see them." And he said, "You got a driver's license or something?" I said, "Yeah. You wanta see it?" He says, "Fine." He looks and he says, "Well, how did you get this fixed?" I said, "What is there to lie about in age?" I said, "I'm 23 years old," you know. And he says, "Well, when you applied here, you put down that you were 20 years old—you know, whatever then—17 or something—now you're 20." And I said, "You're wrong." I said, "Well, let me see the records." "I'm not gonna look for them right now." And I says, "You're mistaken." I says, "All right, when you—." I says, "If you want to make a note, let me change it." He says, "Well, why did you lie?" I says, "Show me them. If it's my handwriting, I lied," I says, "But I don't recall any reason for doing that." And he said, "You're lying." And I just looked and I said, "Don't talk to me like that. I didn't lie," you know. And I says, "Give me the records and I'll change them or talk to the guy who copied it—whatever." I said, "But, you know, let me straighten it out." "You're not 23." I said, "Forget it." And I just walked away and sat down. And this guy says, "What was he carrying on about?" I told him and he says, "Just tell him, you know, to mind his own business." So he comes back and he says, "I wonder what else it was on your records that you lied about." And I said, "Boss," I said, "forget it. If there is something, leave it for Monday." I said, "Because I could tell you're not in the mood to discuss it." And that was it. So Monday came and I says, "Do you want to take a look at my records—can I take a look at my records?" "No. I found out you were right." And, you know, I says, "Forget it," you know, and this guy that he works with says, "All that hassle."

A: Why did you say, "Forget it"? At that point, I mean. . .

P: When I— oh, I said— I was going to say something to him, like, "Why did you carry on like that?"

A: Mmm-hmm.

P: And not even bring out the paper or something.

A: Mmm-hmm. Sure. Yeah.

P: So I figured I better keep my mouth shut because if he was in such a mood for, like, three days, that's it, you know. I don't want to get him all started again over something that wasn't that big anymore. But it was how he kept going on and on like that and I, you know, I asked him—I said, "Why are you picking on me like this?" And I— at first, I looked around and I says, "Maybe it's just me." Maybe I'm taking it too seriously and he's just goofing around or maybe he really is picking on me. But why is he picking on me about jeans or how old he thinks I am?

A: This just started last week, suddenly?

P: Yeah. It was. . .

A: That day? Last Wednesday?

P: Like, Wednesday. Yeah. But Thursday and Friday, he was—fireworks—and, you know, I sat there trying to figure out if I noticed that with anybody else—anything about it. So I asked this girl—I says, "Is he getting on your back about anything?" And she says, "I've taken three rolls of DiGel already." She says, "Don't get into it. Don't ask, because I don't want to tell you." And she says, "I thought it was just me too, but he's really going on everybody." Then she says, "Well, if, like, Monday or something—if he doesn't straighten out like that," she says, "I'm gonna have to go tell somebody about it 'cause he's just getting carried away." And I said, "What is it that he's doing to you? Is it about work or is it personal?" She says, "Work." I says, "Well, it seems to me that he's getting down on me more personally." And she says, "Well, here, I'm involved with certain things to do with the work"—that "I'm working really closely with him so that's what he's fighting with me about." She said, "Here he's not doing that much with you, so he can't think of anything about work that he could get down on you about, so he has to do something, you know, personal like that." And I says, "Well, one more thing he does," I says, "that's it." I said, "I'll haul off at him and, you know, tell him off." And I says, "He wants to fight me, fine, but it was in front of all these people: 'You're not 23. How could you say you're 23? You don't look it.' " Then I says, "Well, that's good, if I don't look it. I'm glad to hear that, you know. Thanks a lot." "Don't get smart with me," you know. I thought—"Aw, forget it"—I was ready to just, you know, walk out right then and go home so I wouldn't have to listen to that anymore.

A: So have things, since Monday, been more settled? With him?

P: He hasn't been around that much. But today, before I was leaving, he came back and he saw I had some Lifesavers on my desk, and he says, "Boy, do I have a headache." He says, "Can I have a Lifesaver?" And I says, "Why don't you take some aspirins instead of a Lifesaver?" And he just looked and he said, "Haha, you're real funny." And I said, "Aw, forget it." I said, "You stay in your own little world," you know.

A: What do you make of his saying that? His coming up and saying that—"Boy, have I got a headache."

P: I know—I see this in a lot of people that things are really confused. I know it's getting to people in such a way, but it's like he's really taking it out on everybody.

A: What is he doing when he's saying, "Boy, do I have a headache"?

P: Just— I don't know.

A: I mean, why did he do that?

P: [pause] I don't know it if was, like, an excuse or something.

A: For what?

P: Like, if he was going to say something like—"Well, don't pay attention to it, I really have a headache," you know. But he didn't. . .

A: Don't pay attention to what?

P: If he was gonna say anything, 'cause I just—you know. I says, "Well, why don't you take some aspirins?" And he says, you know, "Ha, aren't you funny?" And I just walked away right away and he was, like—in a way, the look on his face—like he was gonna start in about something so I just figured I better walk away.

A: Start in about— you— you're, you're— you imagined what kind of thing?

P: Something to do with the work. "Why isn't this done?" Or, you know: "How come you're not doing something?" I don't know. But that's how he's been with just about everybody.

A: "Boy, do I have a headache" sounds like starting a conversation or a, uh— doesn't it? An excuse to talk about something other than work.

P: He doesn't— he's only done that with— well, trying to start a conversation—he's done that once or twice but not much. He's never been. . .

A: Or trying to be friendly.

P: He might have been. . .

A: To, to, uh— uh, smooth over what's gone on between the two of you, sort of— to stop the anger feeling—tension.

P: I don't know. [laugh]

A: To stop the tension. But you're— if— I mean, that's conceivable that that's what that meant. I don't know. It could mean other things, but, but "Boy, do I have a headache" certainly isn't critical of anything you're doing, and it's, uh, sort of just a kind of chit-chatty kind of thing. And Lifesavers go in there somewhere, but you chose to perpetuate the — in the event, that was kind of reaching out to make it— to make up, sort of, you chose to perpetuate the tension.

P: Yeah.

A: 'Cause you were mad.

The therapist's purpose in making this interpretation is not clear.

It may be that he feels unforgiving about the patient's apparent-ly rather cavalier cancellation of the preceding session and is projecting his anger onto her. He seems to be implying that she should not have been, or at least remained, angry—as perhaps he feels, preconsciously, that he should not still be angry with the patient. At the same time, he probably does betray some anger in this critical remark.

P: Mmm-hmm. It was like—for what I felt that how I was re-acting to him Thursday and Friday, you know, like my stomach knotting up right away, I was sitting there, you know, looking at him, seeing him walk in my direction and my stomach would just go, you know, ugh—. Keep your mouth closed, you know. And here he was coming again and I felt like—ohhh, he's gonna do the same thing. . .

A: Mmm-hmm.

P: And, 'cause it seemed like, every afternoon, that's his thing, so I figured. . .

A: So you weren't going to. . .

P: . . .instead of sit there and feeling like that, get up and walk away and you won't even know what happened there, so you won't have to feel like that again, you know, and if he was gonna do that or not, you know. But he might have tried, yeah. He seemed like he was in a little bit better mood today but it — he then — in the afternoon, someone had called for him, and he's supposed to go out of town tomorrow, and I says, "How long are you going for?" And he said, "Just Thursday." And I says, "Aw, that's too bad." I says, "I thought we could get rid of you for two days." And he says, "Well, I probably won't be in Friday," you know. And I said, "Geez, you know, what a job." And I said, "Where you going?" And he said, you know, "To one of the other bran-ches." And I says, "Oh, that's nice." And I was saying, "Oh, that's nice for you," but I was saying—"Oh, that's great for us"—'cause now, you know, it seemed like Monday, Tues-day, and Wednesday was the climax of the week of, you know, relaxing after the weekend. Monday and Tuesday, the days went fine. Wednesday was just starting to build up, and Thursday and Friday, he was like a bear, and here it comes, Thursday and Friday again, and I'm thinking, you know, "Oh, I'm glad he's gonna be gone 'cause then maybe things will be a little bit more relaxed around here."

A: Could we go back to when he asked you to stay late? How did you feel about missing the appointment here?

The therapist has apparently been biding his time, perhaps waiting for some possibly allusion to the missed appointment. Failing to see any that he can plausibly use, but persuaded that the event should be discussed, he returns to it directly.

P: [pause] Well, after— I was— the way he said it, I was scared, like, well—maybe this is what you better do.

A: Stay?

P: 'Cause he seemed—like, the kind of mood he's in—that he'll come down on you tomorrow, so if you do stay today and get whatever you can out of the way, it won't be like that tomorrow.

A: Mmm-hmm.

P: And I thought—well, maybe I could take it home and do it later on tonight so I could make the appointment too—and there was no way I could do that. I would have had to bring a few different books home. So I says, well, I says, "Does it really have to be done?" And he says, "Yeah. I'd really like it done." And I thought—well, it was like making sure the next day would be a little bit better over there. You know, I'd give up one thing for myself to try to help something else.

A: I guess, I'm wondering, to what extent you thought you were really giving something up. You said you were doing him a favor—not much of a favor, just a little favor. That sounds like just giving a little something up.

P: [pause] Well, that could be. [pause] It—no, it was like what I was giving up, doing him somewhat of a favor—not much of a favor—it wasn't, it doesn't, it didn't seem to be like something that was really important. You know, it was like something that someone would like to have done but it wasn't a necessity to be done.

A: Which thing?

P: The job that he gave me to do.

A: Yeah.

P: So it was...

A: Well, I'm asking about the other side of that situation, which is the extent to which the therapy — this appointment — was really important.

P: Yeah.

A: OK. 'Cause I thought — if you say it was only a little favor...

P: No. That was about the kind of work it was.

A: Yeah.

P: No. Not against this, you know.

A: [pause] Well, I guess, there still is a question in my mind about how really important this feels to you —. Or how — just how important it feels to you.

P: Sometimes it, it does feel good being here, you know — what I feel I get out of it — but other times because I try to — I'm, I know I'm more aware of feelings in different things that I do but sometimes I don't understand the feelings or — I can't figure out how to say it — I'm really aware of many things now. Sometimes I think too aware. That I'm so aware of trying to — I'm noticing feelings all the time that I might be, like, confusing feelings, and then I'm not — like, I notice that when I'm talking about things, I describe — like, how bad I felt, but it's how bad did I really feel? I'm not sure of that.

The therapist explicitly asks whether by a "little favor" the patient implied that the session was not very important. She denies this, but her denial is not very convincing. The therapist persists and the patient responds with evidence that the sessions may be upsetting her. So the possibility that she used her boss' request as an excuse to cancel is opened.

A: Mmm-hmm. What are you feeling right now? You — is there some feeling you're having right now as you're saying that?

P: I, I don't understand it that much.

A: I guess, I, I thought I was detecting something in your voice.

P: Oh, shaking like that.

A: Yeah. Which started when you started talking about this. Do you know what that's about? It wasn't there, I don't think, when you were describing the events that went on between you and the boss.

P: Mmm-hmm. No. It didn't.

A: It started when I said, uh, when I started asking about how important the therapy is to you.

The reason for the therapist's asking the patient how she is feeling "right now" becomes clear. He picked up a nonverbal cue that she had become anxious.

P: Oh—. Mmm-hmm. Yeah. I do feel that there's a progress but because I feel that— since I can't really distinguish certain feelings, like, maybe I'm not being honest enough or something. I'm not sure what it is.

A: Mmm-hmm. And how does that touch on— that's interes——, that's important for us to understand better, what you just said, "I'm not being honest enough." What do you mean by that?

The therapist does well to ask the patient to explain what is unclear in this manifest remark. Before one can examine what is latent one must be clear about what is meant on a manifest level.

P: [pause] It is, uh—when I'm trying to describe something. Like, if I'm trying— if I feel scared about something, why don't I just say that? I think I just say—well, I felt a little funny—but why couldn't I just say I really felt scared?

A: Mmm-hmm.

P: Uh, when I talk about T [boyfriend], I know that I still— I know I do feel close to him, uh, and I know I'm still, like, protecting myself of being too close, but I cannot describe exactly how I feel. And when, like, uh, last week, we were talking and he said, "There are—." He said, "All the people that I've gone out with. . ." He says, "I've always had an idea in my head—a picture of someone I would like to meet."

He says, "So many people that I met fitted the picture more towards physical looks but not, like, the inner things about them." He says, "Then I started to wonder about it and found out that the physical looks shouldn't be like that. It's the inner things instead." And he said, "I had to put aside what I wanted somebody to look like and just go by what I wanted them to do for me and me for them." And he says, "I thought I saw that in so many different people." He said, "But I really see that in you." And just the way he said it, I just stopped and said, you know, "That's beautiful." And it was like — can you say the same thing to him or what can you say to him? And I started to cry, like, I felt somehow I'm not giving him enough.

Although it is true that the patient is talking about her feelings about her boyfriend rather than continuing with the subject of whether the therapy is important to her, the move to this more obviously important issue in her life is striking as is the increased affective involvement. The therapist should, according to the principles we advocate, be looking for how the associations about her boyfriend are a continuation of the transference by allusion.

A: OK. And you feel like crying now.

P: Yeah.

A: And I think that you have kind of— the shaking in your voice has been there for a couple of minutes now and, in a way, that's been a feeling like crying all along. It started when I said, "How important is the therapy to you?" And I don't think that, immediately, at that moment you felt tearful about the relationship with T. I'm not sure, but it was so immediate, like a reaction to starting to talk about that.

P: Mmm-hmm.

A: It seems to me that maybe what happened was: something like what happened with T happened with me because I gave you the feeling, right at that moment, like I wanted more from you. Like, I wanted this relationship to be more important to you than maybe it seemed like it was 'cause you missed an appointment.

P: Yeah.

A: And maybe you felt kinda like you were inadequate in some way, at that point, or— and also criticized for not. . .

P: No. Inadequate sounds closer to it.

A: Inadequate.

The beginning of the interpretation—that the patient felt the therapist wanted more from her—may have been influenced by his actual disappointment about the patient cancelling with so little evidence of regret. The interpretation is probably grounded in a conscious countertransference response, which the therapist speculates is also attributed to him by the patient. Adding to the plausibility of this speculation is the fact that a bit of overt behavior on his part, namely, his making an issue of the cancellation, has provided a basis for the patient's drawing this very conclusion about what the therapist is feeling. The associations about the boyfriend, however, refer to the patient's sense of inadequacy, not to anything the boyfriend is demanding. The therapist ends up focusing on this aspect of the patient's experience in the transference and the patient agrees.

P: But it's, uh [sigh], not only to you or him, but it's to me too, I think. More to me. [pause] Like, in a way, I'm— I don't know. I think sometimes that I want to share so much, but yet, I think I should save something for myself —for me, you know—that somebody doesn't know about.

A: Yes. That fits with, uh, the fact that a couple of weeks ago, we talked— right at the end, you brought up the— I asked you something. . .

P: Mmm-hmm.

A: . . .about your sexual relationship with T, and then you told me that you had had intercourse with him, and then I wondered how come you hadn't mentioned it sooner, right? That sounds like maybe one of those things that you were holding for yourself.

The patient introduces a conflict between sharing and withholding. The therapist proposes a concrete instance in the therapy in which he feels she withheld from him. He could have interpreted the cancelled session as a withholding too.

P: Yeah. In a way, uh, I think that day was something about — because I was — the way it happened and, uh — it was not planned or anything and it turned out to be very nice — that I wanted to, like, spend more time talking about it. And enjoy talking about it. It was just, like, I knew that I was running out of time and why . . .

A: Oh, but then that doesn't explain it — you could have, uh, talked about it sooner in the session.

P: [inaudible]

A: And it sounds like an important enough thing, to you, so that it would be precisely the kind of thing you would choose over — . I don't remember exactly what we talked about — but I suspect it would be important to you emotionally, more important emotionally than what we did talk about, in some ways.

P: Yeah.

A: And therefore, it seems to fit what you just said — your idea — that, that maybe it was something that you both wanted to talk about and wanted to hold back, right?

P: Mmm-hmm.

A: And you also feel you've been depriving yourself of something when you hold back and yet, on the other hand, it seems to be working that way that you want to hold things back for yourself.

P: Yeah.

The patient rationalizes her withholding but the therapist persists. Then he empathically focuses on the conflict rather than simply accuse her of withholding.

A: Even if you lose something by it. Almost as if you lose more by sharing it — you're scared somehow.

That she is scared is a new idea, but surely plausible enough to warrant his introducing it. Also, the patient did refer to feeling scared earlier (p. 192), in giving an example of the sort of thing she has difficulty saying.

P: Well, one thing is, I remembered how hard with D [first boyfriend] I tried; I was always the talker. I would try to pull conversation out of him, most of the time, and I felt like I was really confiding in him all the time, and then I'd stop and think — well, when he talks to me, it sounds like he just talks to me and that's it — not really talk, you know. I tried figuring out a way of how I could get him to really open up to me and I couldn't, and I had to take it as — that's how he is. You're this kind of person that you get close to him that you'll tell him whatever you feel. . .

A: Yeah. . .

P: And then when I got kicked in the ass and left standing there, I thought, you know, all that you went through — for what?

A: Mmm-hmm.

P: And I know that after that, I was trying to protect myself from letting that happen again.

A: Well, I think that that's, uh, repeated, in a way, with me. . .

P: Yes.

A: Because I don't tell you, confide in you about my feelings. Even though you might not expect that because I'm a therapist and so on, still the fact is, emotionally, for you, that's the situation, right? You confide in me. You're called upon to confide in me and I'm not called upon to confide in you.

P: Right.

A good example of what we advocate. The associations about the boyfriend are interpreted in terms of the transference, though with no implication that the feelings about the boyfriend are not justified in their own right. Furthermore, the therapist points to what in his own behavior makes her experience of the relationship reasonable from her point of view.

In addition to this interpretation of displacement, an allusion to the transference by identification is a possibility. Perhaps the patient thinks the therapist feels he is vainly trying to get her to open up and now, informed of the ease with which she has sacrificed an appointment, feels he has been "kicked in the ass and left standing."

A: And it might add to your feeling that you should hold it back and reserve certain feelings, and maybe in some way you'll get hurt if, for example — to pick up on what we talked about today, uh, what happened today — if something came out about how you missed having the appointment or if you let yourself feel that and acknowledge it, then it would be giving too much. You could get hurt if that happened 'cause it could turn out — and you sense that it might turn out — that the relationship would become more important to you than it is to me or something.

She has not said she missed having the appointment. The therapist probably wishes she had missed it. More likely she feels she deprived him and feels guilty about it. The parallel would be to her having said she felt guilty, or at least inadequate, for not having reciprocated her boyfriend's attitude toward her (p. 193, line 11). Nevertheless, the therapist's suggestion is not entirely unfounded. Because of the lack of reciprocity in the relationship, it is possible that the patient disavows feelings of attachment to the therapist. She did say (p. 192, line 31) she was protecting herself against feeling too close to her boyfriend.

P: Mmm-hmm.
A: [pause] So when you're — you were talking about feelings in a way. You were talking about all that went on between you and the boss, right?
P: Mmm-hmm.
A: There were feelings about that, but I think that was easier than something else, right?
P: It doesn't sound like I was expressing — I mean — more exact feelings. I think I'm trying to look inside for deep feelings.
A: But you — I think that you realize — you're sensing that you're, in some way, cutting yourself off from feelings sometimes.
P: Mmm-hmm.

A: Right at this moment, something is more close to you and
    you're expressing more than you do at other times, right?
    And one way, I think, that you do that is by telling the de-
    tails of exactly what each person said to the other person.
    What you sometimes do is describe your behavior and his
    behavior: "And he said and then I said, and then he said
    and then I said," right?

P: Mmm-hmm.

A: And the feelings are kinda there. You can hear it, in a way
    —I can. It's not, like, absent completely, but it's also— it
    sounds like a way you hold back something, right? There's
    two things there: one is that there's something about what
    went on that is actually like you missed the forest for the
    trees 'cause there are all the details and something about
    the gut feeling is missed. And then also there's something
    about just what happens— your feelings about this rela-
    tionship sometimes get lost, and that's really very immedi-
    ate and close and scary maybe.

P: If I know that I can do something about it, but it's mostly
    on relaxing. I know that's— I don't relax enough. I don't
    know how much that means, but I, I know I do that.

A: You're sort of on guard.

The therapist's intent is not entirely clear. He apparently wants
to make the general point that the patient is guarded in expressing feelings, especially about him, and that she demonstrates
her guardedness by her reporting of relatively unimportant details. But this general statement may well have the disadvantage
of deflecting the patient from the specific reason for her guardedness, which was being explored.

P: Yeah. [pause] But I noticed that with T— I mean, to me,
    it seems like progress. I look at how I— I felt that right
    from the beginning I was really relaxed with him. I was.
    But now I noticed that it's a lot better. But I know that
    there is still more. That there are certain things that I'm
    still, you know, back off about. But with that, I look at it:
    You've only known this person so many months and you're
    getting to know him better and better so, with certain

things you loosen up here and there — give it time — that's it. But I—. Like, about how I felt, how scared I was of him — to have anything physical. And then one day, I was — we'd gone out and my parents were at some dance and I knew they were going to be gone a long time, and we'd gone out to dinner and came back and it just happened. And after that, I stopped and thought: "All that time you were really scared about it being planned or something and then you didn't even think about it. It just happened. You didn't think about, well, if somebody came home or why not just go to a motel or something. It didn't matter." It was the thing I wanted to do right then. And I felt very comfortable, and I stopped and, you know — . Look it, all this time, how — . I kept thinking: "You're scared, you're scared. Why?"

A: Mmm...

P: And then it just happened. I thought: "That was dumb, you know. It was so easy and it turned out to be really nice, why were you so afraid of it?" And then I know once I — I came out and told him that — I, I remember it happening with D, uh — that first, there can be relationships that start out physical before anything mental, and I said, "That is not for me." I know it would never work for me. So here I would rather have it work the other way around. But who is to say, "How much can you get to know that person before you have any kind of physical relationship?" And it was like I wanted to make sure that the mental part of it was OK, then allow physical, but if I put physical too soon, that might have blown it, for some reason. Maybe that's all you would have then, is physical, and what good is that?

A: Mmm...

P: You know, if you push it too soon, then probably something's gonna go wrong.

A: Mmm-hmm.

P: So just leave it as it was, and as it turned out, it was fine. You know, it was at the right time. And after that, you know, he says, "You know, I really can't believe how, all of a sudden, you reacted that way." And I says, "Well, it was the right thing for me at the right time," you know.

A: Mmm-hmm.

P: And he said, "I'm really glad." He says, "I hope that the other time, you know, when I had— we talked about— that I was pushing you or anything." He says, "No." He says, "I'm, you know— it's not like years and years went by or anything." He said, "It turned out just perfect." And that's how I felt about it then.

A: Mmm-hmm.

P: That, you know, I was kinda scared at first. You know, why are you waiting so long? You know. Nothing— what are you, you know, what are you protecting about it? And that's what it turned out to be, and then after that. . .

A: What do you mean, "That's what it turned out to be"?

P: That I felt I was, you know, putting too much of a hold on anything physical 'cause, you know, I'm protecting so it won't be more physical.

A: Mmm-hmm. You're kinda afraid then that he—either he or both of you—or maybe more he—will be only interested in the physical side.

The patient's associations in response to the general interpretation about guardedness are about how the initiation of sex with her boyfriend turned out well because it had not been hurried, even though she wonders what she was afraid of. The allusion to the transference may be that she is warning the therapist not to push her too quickly to express herself more openly. The therapist does not pick up a possible allusion to the transference at this point; instead, his attention is caught by the manifest associations that she fears her boyfriend may be interested in her only physically. Here a possible allusion to the transference may be that she feels the therapist is interested in her only for the research recording of her sessions.

P: Yeah. Like, that's all that's gonna be then. That nothing else will amount out of it.

A: And that you'll just be a kind of sex object.

P: Yeah.

A: Mmm-hmm.

P: I don't know how much— I think a little bit for me. But I think I was afraid of more that he would do that to me. Or I might— instead of at times— because I said "no" before — like, now, OK, you did relate to him now, you can't say "no" all the time, but I can, you know. It's: Why do I have to say "yes" all the time? Or just like, uh, when I want to go somewhere—some days, I'll feel like doing certain things and other days, no. So that's all right.

A: You mean, you're afraid that once you say "yes" once...

P: Yeah. That everytime...

A: ...you'll never be able to say "no."

P: Yeah.

A: You'd be in one of those— another version of one of those grooves you're afraid you're going to get into and never going to get out of it. Once you go in one direction— we've talked about this in other ways...

P: Yeah. Mmm-hmm.

A: You're afraid you're going to be closed in and trapped and have no way to change. I mean, to vary.

P: Yeah. Right. It was funny—I know there's more to do than just that. For awhile, because you're learning about each other and that, in that area now, so you want to do that more. And you know, it'll slow down a little bit.

A: How can we, uh, relate this to your being on guard with me? Because it seems like here the apparent issue is being on guard with certain feelings, right?

P: Mmm-hmm.

A: And, uh, almost as though something is gonna be lost once you express them. Maybe you'll end up being used in some way or— it almost seems as though it's like the relationship becoming physical. It's almost like that.

The therapist tries to find an allusion to the transference in the preceding associations but is not very clear. He does suggest that the theme of exploitation may be involved, but the idea that something will be lost or that she fears the relationship with him has a physical implication does not seem to hit the mark. Perhaps what he is getting at and what would be more precise and cogent at this point is that the *anxiety* about expressing feelings directly in the therapy is similar to the anxiety the patient has felt about sexual expression in her relationship with her boyfriend.

P: [pause] Well, it—. [pause] Sometimes it's like, if you talk and talk about everything that's on your mind, you have to, like, say something because, what if you happen to run out of something one day to talk about? What am I gonna do? Sit? Not say a word?

A: Mmm-hmm.

P: That's—I don't know—that's...

A: That's part of it then...

P: Yeah.

A: That you have to hold onto some things. But that's similar too, because it's like in sex, it's as though this is your last card that you have to play and that once you play it, you'll have nothing left, right? And it, it somehow is like: And that's all there will be, and it'll somehow, it'll be over—there'll be nothing else. You're afraid, somehow, it'll be finished if you express some kind of feeling about...

P: Yeah. In some way. Uh, I know that from there your feelings can grow, but how much?

A: Hmm. Right. That's where you're scared. You're scared that—. 'Cause you associated it with, uh, not with it growing. You know that intellectually, but you associate with it ending. Right?

The therapist's idea is plausible. She has indeed said something similar about the consequences of having sex (p. 200, line 33). However, he might have done better to first clarify the manifest meaning of her remark about running out of things to say.

P: Yeah. Because of that happening before. I felt that here I was engaged, and I felt that, you know, I really cared for someone a lot, and all of a sudden, they decided that after them knowing you eight years that they didn't want to get married. They wanted to be free and...

A: And it's almost like knowing you more is what— like, they get finished with you when they know you thoroughly — then there's no more.

P: Right. Like that.

A: What I mean by that is that you gave everything of your-
     self and then they found that that was— they used that and
     then went on. That's not quite it.

P: No. [pause] Don't know the right words for it. [pause]

A: But you had the experience of being hurt, right? And that
     much— there's some aspect of it that's not quite in the
     words but we know we got that.

P: Mmm-hmm.

A: But I imagine that that was not the first time, you know, in
     that, uh, that had it's—. My hunch is that that was a repe-
     tition of something too, even though it may— it stands out
     in your mind as the time when you would have been hurt.
     All the symptoms you were having, even before the break-
     up with D, we know they were partly because you were
     scared it would happen.

P: Mmm-hmm.

A: Still they had a particular form in all the tension and the
     buildup and not knowing what the feelings were, and they
     got translated into physical kinds of feelings almost. That,
     in itself, sounds like being afraid of [?] . . .

P: Yeah.

A: Mmm. [pause] One, uh—. I mean, sure it's complicated—
     there's a whole lot of things in your past that go into it—but
     I keep— I've been reminded again of your experience of
     your— of curling up in bed and your father approaching,
     and being scared and feeling like he was getting closer and
     closer and you had no way out, and you had no way to
     avoid it, right? And yet, it ends up being something that's
     half, at least, pleasurable in a way.

P: Mmm-hmm.

A: And all of that has the same, almost the same process in it
     that you described about what went on between you and
     T. It turns out not to be so bad as you would think it is if
     anyone saw you the way you were clutching at that pillow,
     right?

P: Yeah.

A: Also sounds like something that was repeated, in a small
     way, when your boss was approaching the desk and you
     were getting those knots in your stomach. That sounds like

a repetition of that experience—his getting closer and closer and, like, you're crowded in there.

P: Mmm-hmm.

A: But there's some mixture, some conflict about it. It was back then, right?

P: Mmm-hmm.

A: Wanting something and being very afraid of it, and there is now. It has the same form—the conflict—the same feelings are in it, I think.

P: Mmm.

A: Being afraid of something very close 'cause it's mixed with getting hurt as well as with getting something good—being touched.

The therapist has suddenly become excessively active and is overwhelming the patient with interpretations. He brings in genetic material, tries to tie in the earlier part of the session about the boss, and ends rather lamely with a vague statement about fearing closeness because it is dangerous as well as desirable. Why he has left the field of the transference we do not know. It is possible that his behavior represents a countertransference compromise. On the one hand, he backs away from interpreting the transference in the here-and-now in order to avoid an enactment of the kind of interaction he is describing. On the other hand, the ambitiousness of his extra-transference interpretation may, in itself, bear some similarity to the kind of approach the patient fears.

P: But I think it's mostly to do with feeling that you're giving all you could and, like, getting nothing in return—just like a slap in the face and getting hurt all over again. And now, I, I don't think that T would do that, but it's like the same thing. I didn't think D was that kind of person and then he did do that. I— he did show signs of it by, here and there, things he did hurting me. And when I'd tell him about it, he'd say, you know, "I don't want to hear about it." So it's—. I sat back and I was looking—thinking about things he did like that and looking at T and saying, "He's not showing any signs like that," you know.

A: Yes. I know. You were, in fact, telling me a great deal about how he's just not the same. It doesn't make sense, right?

P: Right.

A: And he's giving a lot. And so on. But on a gut level. . . .

P: But I can't believe, in a way, that I am being this lucky. I do feel very lucky to have come across someone like him, and it's now: Will I be able to give enough to him? And it's, you know: I try like— but is that enough? You know. Will he be happy with that much? When he talks about how he feels and that, it sounds like he's really happy. I don't see him crabby or anything, and when he has been, it had to do with, you know, something happening to him at work or something. But he always says, "If there's something that I feel isn't going right, I'll open up about it right away so don't worry about that." And I keep thinking, you know, "This is really a change." For him to sit there and say, "Yes. I will be talking to you. I will confide in you." And I'm going, you know— after having somebody that you had to pull or try to pull it out of, here you're getting it just naturally.

A: Mmm-hmm.

P: And it's, you know, it's such a good feeling to not have to fight with somebody, in a way, for there to be even that bit of closeness, and here I was engaged to that person.

A: Mmm-hmm.

P: Spent, on and off, eight years with him, and I couldn't get that out of him. And here, this person, just four months or so, and I'm getting it so spontaneously, you know. It's really something. And I notice so many different things everyday—not only in him but in me—how I react to him.

A: You have, uh—we have to stop—you have really, in a way, a dilemma because either you're afraid that you're going to be used or you're not gonna get much or you're gonna be hurt or— which doesn't fit with the way T is, but that's one fear. Or he is really the way he is and then you're very scared that you're not good enough.

P: Yeah.

A: And that you won't be able to give enough yourself.

P: Yeah.
A: And then both are scary.

The therapist picks up the theme of getting and giving, and whether she is giving enough. It was introduced much earlier when, in response to the therapist's explicit inquiry about the missed appointment, the patient brought up her fear of being unable to respond adequately to her boyfriend. The therapist dealt well with that by exploring her experience of the relationship, which led to the clarification of her feeling that it was too one-sided. Beginning with his generalized comment that she was guarding herself, however, he interpreted more and more vigorously, with less and less input from the patient. Now, at the end, the theme of getting and giving has returned, albeit not in the transference. Had he continued to focus on her experience of the immediate interaction, it is likely that more would have been accomplished.

P: Yeah. Before it was I was giving and that person wasn't and I left it at that. And here, it seems like both are giving and I should be very happy with it—why not?
A: Mmm-hmm. We have to stop.
P: Goodnight.
A: Goodnight.

ADDITIONAL COMMENTS

Perhaps a central feature of this session is a subtle oscillation in the patient between a fear that the therapist will find her inadequate and withdraw from her and a concern that he is, or will be, hurt by her withdrawing from him. In this connection, the session contains an interesting example of associations that probably allude to the transference via displacement and identification at the same time. As we already noted (p. 196), in speaking of her feelings about being rejected by her first boyfriend, the patient may be alluding simultaneously to her fear of rejection by the therapist (displacement) and to her suspicion that he feels rejected by her (identification). The coexistence of the two mechanisms is probably not uncommon.

PATIENT I: SESSION 111

INTRODUCTION

The following session is of special interest in that it demonstrates the applicability of systematic analysis of the transference to psychotherapy with a schizophrenic patient. In this session, the patient reports hallucinating on three separate occasions. In each case, the fact that the patient hallucinates, and even the content of the hallucination, seems to have meaning in relation to the immediately preceding behavior of the therapist, although the therapist often fails to fully grasp these implications. In general, the therapist works hard to focus on the patient's experience of the interaction. Yet often he seems to strongly affect that experience in the process of interpreting it, without fully recognizing that he is doing so.

THE ANNOTATED SESSION

[two minutes, 40 seconds elapse before patient enters]
P: So?
A: So?
P: You got a bill for me?
A: I do. Yeah. Here it is.
P: [pause] All right. [pause] I didn't bring my pay —— , checkbook today.
A: It's OK.
P: And next week, we're off. So in two weeks, I'll bring the check.

A: OK. [pause] Did you want to reschedule next week's appointment?

This offer seems gratuitous. It behooves the therapist to examine the patient's ensuing associations to see whether they allude to how the patient feels about the offer.

A: [pause] There's one time when I could —. I don't know if you'd be able to because you'd have the same, uh...
P: 'Cause of work.
A: Yeah.
P: What time is it anyway?
A: Thursday at four. [pause] Yeah. Thursday at four.
P: I don't know. [pause] I went to my parent's house for services.
A: [short pause] Why are you shutting your eyes?

The therapist here gives precedence to a nonverbal communication which, presumably, reflects something about the patient's immediate experience of the relationship.

P: I feel uncomfortable.
A: Can you describe that a little more? What do you mean?
P: I always close my eyes when I feel uncomfortable. [pause]
A: Well, what's your discomfort about?
P: [sigh or yawn] [pause] Everything keeps repeating itself.
A: That's an obscure statement, isn't it?
P: You mean, you need more explanation, right?
A: Well, did you expect me to understand it?

The therapist does not want to allow lack of clarity in the manifest content of the patient's associations to pass by without comment.

P: No. I remember when I was first hospitalized here —. My mother was real worried about me and she crawled on top of me. [pause]
A: She crawled on top of you? What do you mean? [pause] Quite literally?

P: Well, I was standing there and she was standing next to me.

A: And she did what?

P: She tried to cover me up.

A: Cover you. From, from what?

P: I don't know.

A: You don't know. Now is that — was that a continued explanation of what you meant by everything keeps repeating itself? How? What's repeating?

P: That at services, she wouldn't leave my seat. [pause] I was sitting in the back row 'cause I didn't have a ticket and F's [brother] in the seat next to me. One seat in between us.

A: Mmm-hmm.

P: And she came back to visit, and I said, "Could you please go? Leave. You make me nervous." And she wouldn't leave.

A: That's the repetition?

P: Yeah.

A: That she crowds you that way? Sort of smothering like? But now why would that make you feel uncomfortable right now, and when you're sitting right here?

P: Because that's what I was thinking about outside.

A: Does that explain it? That's what you were thinking about outside?

P: Out here while I was waiting for you.

A: Right. Then you came in, so why would that explain your — ? It seems to me that you would only be that uncomfortable that you were closing your eyes because you were uncomfortable about something right here in our relationship.

P: I am too.

The therapist's insistence on focusing on the patient's experience in the here-and-now seems worthwhile. However, it introduces the possibility that in the process of being persuaded, the patient may feel dominated or overpowered — perhaps crowded as he felt crowded by his mother.

A: OK. So let's get to that, maybe.

P: Maybe. [laugh]

A: Maybe, huh? [laugh]

The "maybe" appears to be a half-hearted attempt by the therapist to undo his directiveness. The patient gently mocks him
and there is a moment of shared laughter, at the therapist's expense. This is an example of a moment of interpersonal rapport
and contact that may be very important therapeutically, although it is not subjected to detailed analysis.

P: No. 'Cause I don't enjoy leaving work early, plus the fact
     that tomorrow's even harder 'cause I have to work a full
     day and I'm used to leaving at two.
A: Tomorrow is even harder?
P: 'Cause I don't get off at two, I have to stay until five.
A: Oh. Now, so one of the things that's making you uncom-
     fortable about being here is you had to leave work early?
P: Yeah. And there's this guy there who's asking me all kinds
     of questions like: "How— where were you yesterday and
     the day before?" So I said, "I had the Jewish holiday." So he
     says—he started thinking—he says, "Well, N [male co-
     worker] didn't take off. This guy, N he's Jewish, and he
     didn't take off." So he's just doing a lot of nosing around.

There may be an allusion here to the therapist's intrusiveness.
In addition, there may be a specific connection to the therapist's
earlier offer of a substitute appointment the following week. In
other words, the patient may feel that the therapist, like the guy
at work, is reluctant to allow him to take off a day.

A: Well, I'm still doubtful we hit, hit on it, you know—what's
     making you uncomfortable right now. Although you're
     touching on it maybe a little bit with, you know—"It's hard
     to get away from work." How did you feel about my asking
     you about coming in next week on Thursday?
P: I don't think I can make it.

The therapist returns to the offer he made and the patient responds now with what he perhaps had difficulty saying originally.

A: How did you—? OK. That didn't quite answer my question.

P: [laugh] I felt surprised.
A: You felt surprised, right? Uncomfortable?
P: No.
A: You seemed a little bit hesitant about saying "no" there.
P: [laugh] Maybe a little uncomfortable.
A: Yeah. Come on, be straight.
P: A lot uncomfortable. [both laugh]

Here is another example of persistence by the therapist paying off, at least in terms of a manifest confirmation. Now, however, even more than before, the possibility that the patient feels under pressure to comply in response to the therapist's cajoling, even teasing, manner has to be kept in mind.

A: Because you might have felt like, uh, it was, uh, not convenient for you to come an extra day and yet, it was hard to just say, "No." Could that have been it?
P: Could be.
A: And could I have been, like, sort of a smothering mother, you know — covering you and, you know, sort of crowding you and not leaving you. You know, you thought: Next week is Yom Kippur, it's the week off, so you'll see me in two weeks. Period. Now all of a sudden, you got this additional problem to cope with. You're invited to come on Thursday, you know. Should I or shouldn't I? And I think, at the moment, when you said, "Things keep repeating themselves," that's what was repeating. It was repeating right here with me, that was why you —. I was like a . . .
P: No. I thought of that before.
A: I was like a Jewish mother.
P: No. I thought of that before, though. Outside in the hall. That things were repeating. While I was waiting for you, I was thinking that.
A: OK. But I think it's still possible that you felt very uncomfortable. 'Cause then, on top of that, it happened again right now.
P: [laugh] Yeah.

It is to the therapist's credit that he is not swept away by a sense of generosity in offering the substitute appointment and is able, therefore, to detect a disguised allusion to himself in the patient's portrayal of his engulfing mother. Nevertheless, as we have seen in other cases, there may well be a transference-countertransference enactment of the very issue that is being interpreted, even as the interpretation is made and pursued by the therapist. The patient may indeed have felt "smothered" earlier, when the substitute appointment was offered, but he may also be having a similar experience right now. The transference and countertransference are reciprocal and the behavior of each participant elicits a complementary response in the other. The therapist certainly argues his point aggressively; he does not take "no" for an answer, which undoubtedly increases the likelihood that the patient will feel engulfed and overpowered. On the other hand, the patient's elusiveness probably contributes to the therapist's inclination to be so persistent. His elusiveness may even be unconsciously designed to elicit the therapist's persistence.

A: You think so? The other thing that occurred to me was the bathroom business. Maybe you had some feelings about that.

Bringing up yet another issue at this point certainly seems unwarranted, particularly given the patient's perfunctory "yeah." To determine the validity of the interpretation, the patient should be given more opportunity to respond, whether explicitly or by allusion. By switching immediately to another matter, however related it may be, the therapist seems to be saying, "Good, I got you to agree. I win that round; on to another." (Incidentally "the bathroom business" refers to something that happened before the session.)

P: Well, I didn't want to use the one downstairs. Uh, I don't know—well, they usually don't have soap in that bathroom.
A: Mmm-hmm.
P: And I just— I felt like leaving downstairs as fast as I could. Too many people around.
A: Uh-huh. So you thought you'd use this one, right?

P: Yeah.

A: You didn't know it was gonna be locked, did you?

P: I thought it might be locked.

A: Might be locked.

P: I saw you, I saw you in that room down there...

A: Uh-huh.

P: So I start waiting for you to come out to ask you if I could use it.

A: Were you, uh, uncomfortable about asking to use it?

P: No. But I'm very uncomfortable when I ask my mom to use the bathroom. [laugh]

This may be an implicit confirmation of the therapist's hunch that the patient was, in fact, uncomfortable about asking the therapist whether he could use the bathroom (which also meant asking for the key).

A: [laughing] You're uncomfortable to ask your mom...

P: If I could use the bathroom. [pause] Because she always says "no"...

A: Why would you have to ask her?

P: Because she's always in it. [pause]

A: She's always in it?

P: Yeah.

A: She's always in the bathroom?

P: Yeah.

A: You have to ask her to please leave so you can make use of it?

P: Yeah.

A: And that embarrasses you.

P: It frustrates me.

A: It frustrates you. Well, you're not uncomfortable about asking me.

P: No.

A: Well, I suppose there's a danger then that I've talked you into something that isn't true. But I think you might be even a little uncomfortable about asking me. [laugh] Even though you are saying "no." [pause] Now you're closing your eyes again and you said before that that means you're uncomfortable.

P: Yeah. I'm hearing voices.

A: You're hearing voices right now? And they're — what are they saying?

P: [pause] They're telling me that I'm nervous.

The therapist has good reason to be concerned that he may be talking the patient into something that is not true. The fact that the patient hallucinates at this moment clearly seems to reflect a need to withdraw from the therapist, who has become too overbearing and relentless. In addition, what the voices are saying parallels the very idea with which the therapist has been beating the patient over the head. The therapist has been stubbornly insisting that the patient is "uncomfortable," just as the voices are *telling* him he's "nervous." So the patient has withdrawn from the interpersonal battlefield and retreated to an intrapsychic (and "psychotic") one, where, however, the same struggle is re-created.

P: [pause] B [male friend] called me last night.

A: The voices are telling you that you're nervous. I mean, why would you have — why would that have to be a voice rather than a, just a thought?

P: Because it's my luck. That's the way it goes with me.

A: Well, I don't know what the specific meaning of their telling you that you're nervous is, but maybe, you know — you closed your eyes, right? — and you went like this, and then you said you're hearing voices, and it seemed to me like maybe, right then, something between us was, like, too much. You know, too much. That you just wanted to hide from it. Too much intensity. And the voices sort of sound like they're a little bit of an escape, from our interaction. It's like you got another conversation going, right? We've discussed that before. It's a little bit of a moving away from something right here.

The therapist does well to try to catch the meaning in the immediate interaction of the patient's withdrawal. Unfortunately, he fails to recognize or mention the specific ways in which his own manner of relating has been "too much."

P: I have this fear I'll be hospitalized again.

A: Now, as important as that is—what you just said—and I
    don't want to, I'm not gonna forget you just said that—you
    didn't respond to what I said—at least, not directly.

This is a good example of how the patient's behavior elicits a
domineering response from the therapist. If the patient were al-
lowed to go on to elaborate on this new and undoubtedly important fear of being hospitalized, the fact that he ignored what the
therapist said on a manifest level might get lost, even though the
therapist might be able to detect a latent continuity in the ensuing associations. Indeed, one could already speculate that the
patient may be saying: "Your overbearing manner is driving me
into a psychotic withdrawal which I fear will require hospitalization." Nevertheless, the fact that the patient chooses, on a
manifest level, to ignore the therapist does seem in itself to deserve some comment, even though it continues the enactment of
engulfment.

P: Oh—. Yeah, you know, my father again.
A: No. Do you know what I mean? Your father again? You're
    being obscure. You're doing that. You're not answering—I
    mean, you're not saying—. Do you think that what I said
    was true? That maybe you felt like withdrawing a little bit
    from the relationship here or from our interaction?
P: Yeah. It's true.
A: Am I supposed to understand that that's the case if you just
    don't say anything?
P: Yeah.
A: Well, how would I know?
P: [laugh] How would you know what?
A: How would I know what, what you think of what I said—
    unless you tell me.
P: OK. I'll tell you.
A: [pause] It's another kind of avoidance, I think, of actually
    relating, like we said before. Just change the subject and let
    it go sort of unanswered. Like, I just talked and then, then
    you'll talk [patient laughs] about something that's sort of
    related. Like, if I'm smart enough, I'll figure out the rela-
    tionship between what you said and what I said, you know.

I'm always showing off how I can do that anyway, right?

Here the therapist spells out his dilemma, referring to a pattern of interaction he wants to avoid.

P: Well, when we left services Sunday night, my father—. Listen to this, it'll give you a kick.
A: It'll give me a kick?
P: Yeah.
A: Well, that's important. [patient laughs] Now we've got a few loose ends hanging. One is that you're afraid you're going to be hospitalized. OK. Now we, I haven't forgotten you said that. Now you want to talk about something that happened in services with your father. OK.
P: After services.
A: After services.
P: We were leaving. We were walking toward a car, and I'm going on and on about how if I get married, I want to get married in the synagogue and things like that. Then he says—he points and says—"That man left his lights on in the car." Had nothing to do with what I said, you know.
A: Uh-huh.
P: Right away I started thinking: Dr. J. S. [therapist's name].
A: Uh-huh. Yes. That sounds exactly like the kind of thing I talk about, right. That goes on with us. So who was who? He was acting like. . .
P: Me. And I was you.
A: Right. Right. So we have a little idea about one place that it comes from, right?
P: Well, I could have told you that.
A: You did tell me that, in fact, before, that your father doesn't. . .
P: Does it so often.
A: He just ig——, says something that seems completely irrelevant to what you said and you do that with me.

This is a rather remarkable insight by the patient: that what the therapist experiences with him is like what he experiences with his father. It is also probably perceptive of the patient to realize that his recognition of this parallel will give the therapist "a kick." The connection to the experience with the father seems to be spontaneous and important in its own right, although it also introduces the element of giving the therapist pleasure.

P: I inherited it from him.
A: It's in the genes. Right. It's not your fault.
P: Yeah. It's not my fault.
A: Yeah. What can you do about it?
P: What can I do about it? It's a good question. [pause]
A: You're doing something. You're doing something about it. You're working on it right now. You just responded three times in a row to things I said.
P: Was it three in a row?
A: That's four. [laugh] [pause]

This sort of tongue-in-cheek banter probably is another example of spontaneous rapport that has therapeutic value for this patient (cf. p. 209–210). Nevertheless, there may be a kind of flirtatious aspect to it that should also be examined analytically sooner or later.

A: What was that about, uh, getting scared that you might have to be in the hospital again? What led to that thought? [pause] [patient sighs or yawns] That was a long time ago, huh? Now you. . .

Clearly, the therapist is concerned about having interrupted such a provocative association. Yet to ask the patient to go back to it at this point may compound rather than ameliorate the difficulty he is creating by being so directive.

P: [pause] Well, let me explain something first. Is that OK?
A: Yes. It's good you asked my permission.
P: OK. I got this fear of. . .
A: See, by saying, "Let me explain something first," that already takes care of it, right? Because, at least, you acknowledged that there was something else — right? — that was, that was — that I raised — the question I raised that

you were not responding to. So you're saying, "Let me explain"—because usually you leave that out. You leave that
little phrase out, like, "Wait a second, let me talk about this
first" or "I'm gonna ignore that for a second 'cause I want to
talk about this." You just leave that out and you just, you
don't acknowledge that you're doing it, you know.

P: Could I go on?

A: You realize that? Yes, you can go on. [laugh] I guess I'm
going on quite a bit, huh?

The therapist certainly is "going on quite a bit." His speech
above, whatever its merit, seems not only to ignore the patient's
sarcastic question ("Is that OK?") but ironically continues to ex-
emplify the very thing the patient is being sarcastic about—that
is, the extent to which the therapist takes the initiative.

P: OK. Uh, I have this fear that bills won't be paid. I mean, F
just bought a second car—cost him six thousand dollars.
Had to get it financed and I imagine he won't lose his job—
I have this fear if I undertake something like buying a car,
my job won't last long enough for me to pay it off.

A: Mmm-hmm.

P: Or pay rent for an apartment or something like that. And
everything depends on keeping the job.

A: Mmm. You can't stand that feeling of, of— that you have
to keep the job.

P: Yeah. I imagine that's it. Yeah.

A: Why is it so hard to tolerate?

P: It's hard to imagine that I won't get fired from the job.

A: Why?

P: I don't know. Something is always happening to me on jobs.

A: Mmm-hmm. Did getting the bill now add to, uh— after
all, it's the first time, I guess, I ever handed you a bill—. I
think, right? Did that add to that feeling of responsibility
and pressure and...?

The therapist is alert to recognize the possibility here of a displaced allusion to the transference.

P: No. I don't think so. It's small enough I don't have to worry
about it.

A: It's a small amount but it still might have a meaning to you that you're— that there's certain expectations that you can. . . .

P: Yeah. You hand me a bill and it automatically assumes that I keep my job.

A: Yeah. that's what I mean. Puts pressure on you.

This is yet another example of persistence on the therapist's part leading to a confirmation which may represent compliance.

P: Just living is pressure, for me, anyway. I don't know.

A: Maybe everything is, like, uh, something closing in on you, you know. Like your mother. It's, like, you had the job and you felt good about having the job. It's your job. It was your choice, right? Or at least, it was something you wanted, right?

P: Yeah.

A: But now it's turning into something you have to do and—. Like, you're trapped in it—you know what I mean? The way your mother traps you in her arms or something. You can't breathe.

P: I just heard a voice. They said, "That's on 'What's Happening.' They can't breathe."

This second instance of hallucination in the hour may once again have been precipitated by the therapist's activity, from which the patient feels he needs to withdraw. It is also possible, however, that in this case the therapist's remark hit home and that it was the empathy itself that created a sense of threatening engulfment requiring that the confirmation take the form of a hallucination.

A: That's what?

P: There's a show called "What's Happening". . .

A: Yeah.

P: And the mother's real big and everytime he hugs— she hugs the son, he always ends up saying, "I can't breathe."

It is conceivable that "he hugs" is a slip and that "he" refers to the therapist.

A: Mmm-hmm.

P: I heard that voice just when you said that.

A: Mmm-hmm.

P: It was more than a thought. It was an actual voice in my mind.

A: Uh-huh.

P: If it was just a thought, I probably wouldn't make anything of it.

A: What do you make of it that it's a voice?

P: It's symptomatic of my other voices.

A: Yeah. But it's, uh—. The way it happened, it sounds like it's a way of breathing, you know what I mean? 'Cause if it was just a thought that you would say to me, then we'd be directly in relation to one another, and maybe then you'd feel more like that kid in "What's Happening." But if you have this voice going, it's like, uh, you know, you have something— you know how those kids, kids walk around with radios to their ears. . .?

P: Yeah.

A: They're in their own world a little bit and it shuts out, you know, the outside.

Again, just as in his interpretation after the first hallucination, the therapist fails to call attention specifically to his own behavior as a possible precipitant.

P: I know. That's why I'm not wearing my glasses. I don't want to be so sensitive to everything going on around me.

A: All the stimulation, sort of.

P: Yeah.

A: Mmm-hmm.

P: Take my glasses off on the train. All the time.

A: Mmmmmm. . .

P: Well, not all the time, just when I feel I hear voices.

A: Uh-huh.

P: Either that or I wear shades over them to close my eyes.

A: Mmm-hmm. So that's another meaning of hearing voices maybe, right? It's part of the shutting out of the outside.

P: I remember when. . .

A: It's just in——, it's something just inside yourself, you know.

[pause] Excuse me, "I remember when. . ."

P: Oh, yeah. I was gonna say something. I would say it, you know. I remember one time with, uh, uh, Mr. K — there was exactly one time, when I; he was a counselor at E [vocational school] and I had to see him every, once a week — and there was, like, only one time when I wasn't hearing voices while I was seeing him. He said I hear voices 'cause of my parents. [pause]

A: 'Cause of your parents? 'Cause of what about your parents?

P: 'Cause of everything they put upon me — all the havoc they wreaked with me.

A: Mmm-hmm.

P: [pause] I feel like I'm searching or something when I close my eyes. If I can't find what I'm looking for, I should close my eyes and look further or something.

A: Mmm. You don't have a sense of what it is you're looking for, just that you're looking, sort of. [pause] Do you have the feeling when I'm looking at you that I'm looking for something?

This question seems rather arbitrary.

P: No.

A: [pause] Not that I'm trying to look inside you or something? [pause] [horn blows outside] Now you just, uh, drifted, right?

P: Until I heard that horn.

A: The horn brought you back?

P: I was thinking maybe I could use the bathroom after I see you. Or I could use the one in G [other building].

A: What do you mean? Today? What's this business about the bathroom today? Before *and* after?

P: I got the cramps, that's all.

A: You do?

P: But I don't want to use it now 'cause it'll take up part of our time. [pause] Does that make sense?

A: Yeah. Depending on how uncomfortable you are. Or how much you need to. . .

P: [pause] So you think I'll hear voices on the train going home?

A: Do I think you what?

P: That I'll hear voices on the train going home. [laugh] It's up to you.

A: Is it? [both laugh]

P: Whatever you say.

This comment seems like an unconsciously sarcastic allusion to the therapist's own assumption of control over the patient's life, as reflected in his overzealous interpretations throughout the session and, most immediately, in his control over the keys to the bathroom.

A: That's peculiar. You mean, I could— I have the power to. . .

P: I knew you'd say "power."

A: Huh? You knew I— what did you say? You knew I'd say that?

P: Yeah. [laugh]

A: There's a lot going on here that is quite, uh—what shall we call it?

P: Meaningful?

A: Meaningful for sure, but also, uh, ESP-ish—you know— not ESP-ish, extra——, you know, extra telepathy or something. You knew I was gonna say that and I can say something that will result in your not hearing voices later. I mean, a lot of magic. But do you have that feeling that there's something I could say that would— or were you just kidding?

P: I don't think I was kidding.

A: That there's something I could say—. If I say, "No, I don't think you'll hear voices," you won't?

P: Maybe. [pause] [laugh] Crazy.

A: Gives me a lot of power. [pause] What are you laughing at? The way I raised my eyebrows?

P: Yeah.

A: You're really struggling today, it seems like.

P: Maybe I could use the bathroom now, is that OK?

A: [pause] Yeah. I guess. I can give you the key which— I imagine this whole transaction is some sort of loaded, uh, meaningful business, right? Is it?

P: I don't know.

A: I mean, see, I don't know whether you, you feel you really have to go to the john, or, uh, you're, uh, enjoying the idea of using my key. That's the one, though.

P: Back in a minute. [patient leaves] [after seven minutes, 15 seconds, patient returns] Thanks. [pause] [sigh] I found new freedom; I can use the bathroom whenever I want.

The patient's departure for more than seven minutes surely has psychological significance and transference implications, even granting the reality of the patient's cramps. Now, rather than hallucinating, the patient has physically removed himself from the presence and influence of the therapist. Not surprisingly, when he returns, he speaks of finding "new freedom."

A: Mmm-hmm.

P: No cockroaches. No one saying I can't use the bathroom. [pause] Or "I'll be out in a minute," and it'll be five minutes.

A: You mean, you can use this bathroom now, so you have new freedom?

P: Yeah.

A: No cockroaches—. No— you know, it all sounds like you have now fully moved in.

P: To your apartment?

A: Yes.

P: Yeah.

A: It's like—oh, now we're roommates, you can use the john. You use the same john I use—same bathroom—and, uh, it's a pleasure. It's refreshing, right? Little bit of, like, home to use the bathroom here—. Right?

P: Whose home? Your home.

A: My home. Right. Or, or our home, or something like that. Like, we share it in common. That's the part of it, I guess, that's kind of gratifying to take my key and use the bathroom.

The therapist picks up on only half the story. In leaving the office and, apparently for the first time, using the bathroom on the same floor, the patient expresses *simultaneously* his wish for greater intimacy with the therapist and his need to get away from him. The therapist recognizes the former but ignores the latter — the need to withdraw and the rejuvenating effects of the distance.

P: I didn't need your key. Dr. V [other doctor] was in there.
A: You didn't need it?
P: Dr. V was in the bathroom first. So when he went out, I went it.
A: How did you know he was in there?
P: I knocked on the door.
A: Oh, you knew you should knock first?
P: Yeah. I saw him do that.
A: I see. So now it's turning into a rather — a whole communal [patient laughs], a communal living situation, right?
P: [pause] Are you gonna say it or not?
A: Huh?
P: Tell me I don't hear voices. I want you to tell me that. I didn't hear voices at services until I was made uncomfortable by my mother. Even then I didn't hear voices; I went downstairs. I ran away from her.

He ran away from his mother just as he ran away from the therapist. Perhaps the patient is saying implicitly: "Your pushing me around caused the voices, so you should do something to get rid of them. You got me into this; you get me out of it."

A: I'm rather, uh — I'm still kinda puzzled by, you know, you — your asking, literally asking, me to stop the voices by just predicting that you won't hear them, right? [pause] Yeah. I mean, does that seem reasonable to you?
P: Yeah.
A: Why are you laughing then?
P: [laughing] No...
A: I don't think it does.
P: They gotta go away eventually; they can't be there the rest of my life. I'll make the headlines — front page.

A: Is it, is it...

P: M [patient's name] obsessed by voices. Claims he cannot control them. It's like—R. H. [baseball player] irked by T's [male friend] comment.

A: What did you say? R. H. what?

P: [laughing] I gotta explain that one.

A: Please.

P: [continuing to laugh] It's funny. I got to the ballgame with T.

A: Mmm-hmm.

P: You know, T?

A: Yeah.

P: So everytime we go to the ballgame, he sits in the bleachers and yells at, yells at R. H. for not catching the ball. So he said tomorrow's paper will be the headlines—"R. H. irked by T's torment."

Maybe the patient feels he has been "irked" by the therapist's "torment."

A: R. H. irked by whose torment?

P: Almost said, "Voices." [pause] I almost said, "By T's voices."

A: I see.

P: He called me last night. He wanted me to go to this Recovery thing with him. [pause]

A: You know, uh, the last, uh, three or four minutes—what are you laughing about?

P: I know what you're gonna say.

A: You know what I'm gonna say? What do you think I'm gonna say?

P: We went skipping around, changing subjects a lot.

This seems to be an alert observation on the patient's part. It probably was what the therapist had in mind.

A: And what subject do you think we're avoiding? Can you guess what I—since we're into this sort of reading minds business—...?

P: I don't know. I can't tell you.

A: I think it's a subject that has to do with, uh, uh, going to the bathroom here and using my key making this seem like home. I think that subject. . .

P: Well, I did have the cramps.

A: There's that too, but, uh, I— that, that doesn't nullify the other, right? Could be both.

P: Yeah.

A: You did choose today to, to, you know, wait until you got up here and you did wait to use my key and so on and so forth, right? I mean, that subject is one that you want to, I think, get away from because it's too— it stirs up too much feeling, I think. You think it could be? That it stirs up a lot of feelings?

P: [yawn or sigh] [pause] Yeah. Maybe I should get contact lenses. Then I don't have to wear glasses anymore.

A: Mmm-hmm. That was a quick escape too.

P: Yeah. But it was the same subject, though.

A: How?

P: 'Cause when I wear glasses, I hear voices. When I don't wear glasses, I hear voices but I'm able to deal with them more effectively; I'm able to cope with it as long as I'm not wearing glasses. When I wear my glasses, it scares me.

A: It seems like the whole thing is much more, uh, you're much more preoccupied with it today than you have been. Why? I wonder.

P: It bothers me more.

A: Why? Why is it bothering you more today than it has? I mean, I know it's bothered you before too. But why are you so much more preoccupied today, even talking about needing hospitalization and so on?

P: I didn't say I needed to be hospitalized. I said I had a fear of being hospitalized.

A: Fear. OK. All right. Fear. [pause] You know, the two things seem to go together—that's my impression. The two things being some sense of being more adult and more a man and more responsible and so on. You get a bill, right? That you have to pay. And you want to use the bathroom here, which is sort of a shared thing with me, right? You with me?

P: I don't think I'm sharing with you; I'm sharing with every-
      body.
A: Well, everybody, but I mean, it happens to include me,
      which I don't think is, is, you know, just coincidence, right?
P: OK.
A: My key. Anyway, all those feelings go with some good feel-
      ing about yourself, I think — of sort of participating with
      me and being like a man. And then the opposite thing goes
      on — sort of comes right with it — like, a feeling like you're
      gonna regress and you're very sick and like you're, you
      know — this business about voices is, is gonna overtake
      you, and, and you won't be able to keep your job, and, and
      you're gonna have to be in the hospital, and you get scared
      of all this. It's almost like you feel like you've gone too far
      and you get scared — like you're too high up.
P: [pause] Hearing voices again.
A: What were they now?
P: I don't know. Went by too fast.

Once again the patient hears voices. This time it's after a long
interpretation by the therapist and probably has the meaning,
once more, of withdrawal precipitated by the therapist's mo-
nopolizing and controlling interpretive activity. Even more
striking is what the patient says about the voices — that he does
not know what they said because they "went by too fast." This
surely is a displaced sarcastic allusion to the therapist's long interpretation, which probably went right past the patient and
had little or no meaning to him.

A: [pause] One — there was one other thing we didn't touch
      on and I think it might be important, and that is that you
      saw me in that office when you came in, you know. Maybe
      that — maybe you had a lot of reaction to that.
P: Well, it shows you do something else besides sit in this
      office all day.
A: Yeah. Presumably, I was — did you see that I was with
      someone else?
P: Yeah.
A: Or guess that or hear something. . .?

P: I saw.
A: OK. So when we talked about exclusion once, right? Being something you'd be very sensitive to, right?
P: We talked about that?
A: Yeah. Being excluded. [pause] Anyway, it could have been enough to— that could have been enough to cause some reaction, and maybe that was sort of stimulating.
P: You mean, hear voices?
A: Yeah. As a substitute for something else, that would be even more painful. Like your jealousy of my being in there with, with this other person. [short pause]

Here is yet another example of the therapist overwhelming the patient with interpretations. In this instance, the interpretation he suggests is not supported by any evidence.

A: Well, we have to stop.
P: All right.
A: So now I'll see you in a couple of weeks, right?
P: Yeah.
A: OK.
P: Have a good holiday.
A: You too.

ADDITIONAL COMMENTS

Although working with a severely disturbed patient is likely to place great demands on a therapist and to challenge his personal resources and technical proficiency in special ways, we are persuaded that in many, if not all, such cases the basic principles governing one's approach should remain the same as with less disturbed patients. The session presented here shows that in a psychotherapeutic context, psychotic symptoms can be understood and interpreted as disguised communications about the patient's experience of the immediate interaction. In this case, the patient's concerns, which are about the dangers of being engulfed, and the way in which he deals with them, by withdrawing and hallucinating, undoubtedly reflect the severity and specific nature of his disturbance. Nevertheless, the task of the therapist remains essentially the same as it would be with a neurotic patient: to understand and tactfully interpret however the patient is experiencing the relationship, with particular attention to the contributions of the therapist's own behavior to that experience.

AFTERWORD

We are fully aware that there is a considerable distance between what has been presented here and systematic research that would demonstrate the benefits of analyzing the transference in the manner proposed in Volume I. Although we have developed a coding scheme (Gill and Hoffman, 1982) which makes more rigorous investigation of the phenomena illustrated in these sessions possible, we elected not to apply it here because we thought it might distract the reader from the flow of the clinical material. The scheme, however, did serve as a guiding framework for our annotations, and we hope to make it an integral part of future research on the psychoanalytic process. In the meantime, as noted in the Introduction, our purposes will be well served if this book clarifies the particular technique that we espouse and if it stimulates others in the field, whether in accord with our views or not, to present psychoanalytic data in their original, verbatim form to demonstrate whatever positions they hold.

REFERENCES

Apfelbaum, B. (1965), Ego Psychology, Psychic Energy, and the Hazards of Quantitative Explanation in Psycho-Analytic Theory. *International Journal of Psycho-Analysis,* 46:168–181.

Berger, M., Ed. (1978), *Videotape Techniques in Psychiatric Training and Treatment,* Rev. Ed., New York: Brunner/Mazel.

Dahl, H. (1974), The Measurement of Meaning in Psychoanalysis by Computer Analysis of Verbal Contexts. *Journal of the American Psychoanalytic Association,* 22:37–57.

_____ ; Teller, V.; Moss, D.; & Trujillo, M. (1978), Countertransference Examples of the Syntactic Expression of Warded-off Contents. *Psychoanalytic Quarterly,* 47:339–363.

Gill, M. M. (1976), Metapsychology Is Not Psychology. In: *Psychology versus Metapsychology: Essays in Honor of George S. Klein* [*Psychological Issues,* Monogr. 36], ed. M. M. Gill & P. Holzman. New York: International Universities Press, pp. 71–105.

_____ (1982), An Interview with Merton Gill. *Psychoanalytic Review* (in press).

_____ & Hoffman, I. (1982), A Method for Studying the Analysis of Resisted Aspects of the Patient's Experience of the Relationship in Psychoanalysis and Psychotherapy. *Journal of the American Psychoanalytic Association* (in press).

_____ ; Simon, J.; Endicott, N.; & Paul, I. (1968), Studies in Audio-Recorded Psychoanalysis: 1. General Considerations. *Journal of the American Psychoanalytic Association,* 16:230–244.

Gottschalk, L., & Auerbach, A., Eds. (1966), *Methods of Research in Psychotherapy.* New York: Appleton-Century-Crofts.

Haggard, E.; Hiken, J.; & Isaacs, K. (1965), Some Effects of Recording and Filming on the Psychotherapeutic Process. *Psychiatry,* 28:169–191.

Langs, R. (1978), *Technique in Transition.* New York: Aronson.

Levenson, E. (1972), *The Fallacy of Understanding.* New York: Basic Books.

Lipton, S. D. (1977), Clinical Observations on Resistance to the Transference. *International Journal of Psycho-Analysis,* 58:463–472.

Luborsky, L. (1967), Momentary Forgetting during Psychotherapy and Psychoanalysis: A Theory and Research Method. In: *Motives and Thought: Psychoanalytic Essays in Honor of David Rapaport* [*Psychological Issues,* Monogr. 18/19], ed. R. R. Holt. New York: International Universities Press, pp. 177–217.

Macalpine, I. (1956), The Development of Transference. *Psychoanalytic Quarterly,* 19: 501–539.

Mahl, G. (1960), Disturbances and Silences in the Patient's Speech in Psychotherapy. *Journal of Abnormal & Social Psychology*, 53:1–15.

Racker, H. (1968), *Transference and Countertransference.* New York: International Universities Press.

Rogers, C. (1942), The Use of Electrically Recorded Interviews in Improving Psychotherapeutic Techniques. *American Journal of Orthopsychiatry*, 12:429–434.

Sandler, J. (1976), Countertransference and Role-Responsiveness. *International Journal of Psycho-Analysis*, 3:43–48.

Simon, J.; Fink, G.; Endicott, N.; Paul, I.; & Gill, M. (1970), Studies in Audio-Recorded Psychoanalysis: 2. The Effect on the Analyst. *Journal of the American Psychoanalytic Association*, 18:86–101.

Wallerstein, R., & Sampson, H. (1971), Issues in Research in the Psychoanalytic Process. *International Journal of Psycho-Analysis,* 52:11–50.

Will, O., & Cohen, R. (1953), A Report of a Recorded Interview in the Course of Psychotherapy. *Psychiatry*, 16:263–282.

INDEX

235

ABOUT THE AUTHORS

MERTON M. GILL, M.D., is a graduate of the University of Chicago and the Topeka Institute for Psychoanalysis. He has been a staff member of the Menninger Clinic and the Austen Riggs Center and has taught at Yale University Medical School and the Downstate Medical Center. Currently Dr. Gill is Professor of Psychiatry at the Abraham Lincoln School of Medicine, University of Illinois, Chicago. He is also on the faculty and a supervising analyst of the Chicago Institute for Psychoanalysis. His numerous publications include *Diagnostic Psychological Testing* (with David Rapaport and Roy Schafer), *Hypnotherapy* and *Hypnosis and Related States* (both with Margaret Brenman), *Topography and Systems in Psychoanalytic Theory,* and *Freud's 'Project' Reassessed* (with Karl Pribram). He is also the editor of *The Collected Papers of David Rapaport* and a co-editor of *Psychology versus Metapsychology* (with Philip S. Holzman).

IRWIN Z. HOFFMAN, Ph.D., is a graduate of the University of Chicago and a candidate at the Chicago Institute for Psychoanalysis. Currently he is Assistant Professor of Psychology, Department of Psychiatry, Abraham Lincoln School of Medicine, University of Illinois, Chicago. He is also on the faculty of the Chicago School for Professional Psychology and a consultant for the Psychiatric Residency Training Program for the Illinois State Psychiatric Institute. He is the author of several articles on the mourning process and on psychotherapy. In 1980, he was the first recipient of the Chicago Institute's Edwin Eisler Prize for his paper "Death Anxiety and Adaptation to Mortality in Psychoanalytic Theory" (published in *The Annual of Psychoanalysis,* Volume 7).

PSYCHOLOGICAL ISSUES

PSYCHOLOGICAL ISSUES

HERBERT J. SCHLESINGER, *Editor*

Editorial Board